Multiple Personality and the Disintegration of Literary Character

From Oliver Goldsmith to Sylvia Plath

Multiple Personality and the Disintegration of Literary Character

From Oliver Goldsmith to Sylvia Plath

Jeremy Hawthorn

St. Martin's Press   New York

All rights reserved. For information, write:
St. Martin's Press, Inc., 175 Fifth Avenue, New York, NY 10010
Printed in Great Britain
First published in the United States of America in 1983

ISBN 0-312-55263-7

Library of Congress Cataloging in Publication Data

Hawthorn, Jeremy.
  Multiple personality and the disintegration
of literary character.

  Bibliography: p.
  Includes index.
  1. English literature—History and criticism. 2. Multiple personality in
literature. 3. American literature—History and criticism. 4. Doubles in
literature. 5. Characters and characteristics in literature. 6. Psychology and
literature. I. Title.
PR409.M84H39 1983   820'.927   83-2876

ISBN 0-312-55263-7

For my parents who, fortunately for me, are quite unlike most of the parents described in the following pages

Contents

Acknowledgements

I first developed an interest in many of the themes and issues explored in this book during collaborative work with a psychologist colleague from Sunderland Polytechnic – Peter Hawkins. I owe him my grateful thanks for many insights gained in the course of teaching a syllabus on 'Breakdowns in Communication' with him. Dee Dine provided me with many ideas concerning the work of Jean Rhys, and Deborah Thomas made me acquainted with Nathaniel Hawthorne's *Wakefield*. I also owe very much to students past and present in Britain and Norway. All errors and inadequacies in what follows are, of course, mine alone.

A generous grant towards the cost of printing this book was made by the Norwegian Research Council for Science and the Humanities (Norges Almenvitenskapelige Forskningsråd). I am extremely grateful to the Council for its valuable support in a time of considerable financial constraint.

Acknowledgement is also due to the following owners of copyright material for permission to reproduce extracts in this book: Messrs Harper & Row, New York and Faber & Faber, London for extracts from *The Bell Jar* and the poems by Sylvia Plath; and to Olwyn Hughes for the extract from her thesis, *The Magic Mirror*.

Preface

One of the commonplaces – or clichés – associated with literary modernism is that the human individual is neither unitary nor internally consistent, but complex, contradictory and divided. As Virginia Woolf has Bernard express it, in *The Waves*, 'I am not one person; I am many people.'

In discussing such literary portrayals of inner multiplicity many critics have quoted from Virginia Woolf's essay 'Mr Bennett and Mrs Brown', in which she makes the rather tongue-in-cheek comment that 'in or about December, 1910, human character changed.' We do not necessarily have to accept so precise a date to suspect that such major changes in the view taken of individual human identity by writers must have some basis in a wider social reality. Indeed the more one looks into the matter the more it becomes apparent that the social and literary developments concerned have been in process over a considerable period of time. In spite of a regrettable current tendency to regard the Victorian age in Britain and elsewhere as the period of simple, if not simplistic, realism, during which time literary works portrayed 'reality' as whole, unproblematic and easily accessible, closer study reveals a different picture. Nor is the nineteenth century a time during which the literary character shows no signs of the metamorphosis that is to overcome him or her in December, 1910.

This book started to assume its present form after I had read a number of accounts of multiple personality: cases in which single individuals seemed to be possessed by two or more apparently totally different personalities which were, to a greater or lesser extent, ignorant of one another's existence. I was struck by the fact that there appeared to be analogies and, in some cases connections, between the divisions of personality reported on in these accounts and the divisions within literary characters of which I have already spoken. It seemed to me that bringing together literary portrayals of personality disintegration with such clinical accounts might result in mutual illumination, and might also point towards explanations for both the literary and the clinical fragmentation of personality, in larger changes in the social life of the modern period.

Introducing his edition of Otto Rank's classic text *The Double*, Harry Tucker Jr, after noting that the interest of the reading and listening public is especially drawn to the theme of the double during or just after major upheavals of society, suggests that further inquiry into such apparent connections needs to involve 'skilled and cautious investigation' which, in addition to heeding the work of previous writers on the theme of the double in literature, must include also the information provided by 'political and social history, comparative literature, literary criticism, and psychology.' I have not limited myself to a concern with the literary double in this book, but to the extent that my abilities permit I have tried to bring together the sort of information that Tucker suggests we need to assemble in order to study such complex issues. It seems hardly necessary to add, of course, that in many areas I felt hampered by the limitations of my knowledge and expertise.

It should be clear from the foregoing that I have scant sympathy with formalists, either of the old 'New Critical' variety or of the new Althusserian Marxist species, who argue the pointlessness of trying to establish any links between social life, history and literature. This is not, however, to suggest that I see no problems involved in such an attempt to discover relationships – causal or otherwise – between these areas. There are enormous difficulties involved in trying to establish connections between clinical dissociation, literary accounts of personality fragmentation and division, and larger social and historical processes. Issues of selectivity, representativeness, mediation, influence, genre and interpretation (among others) demand consideration at every stage of the inquiry. I hope that the reader will accept that the lack of any overtly theoretical discussion of such issues does not mean that I have been unaware of them. I have however tried to take account of the difficulties indicated by such complex questions in a concrete way, in the course of considering particular cases and texts.

Daniel Keyes's interesting study of multiple personality, *The Minds of Billy Milligan* (New York, Random House 1981) appeared after I had completed this book. It offers no information which has caused me to question anything I have written, however, and it confirms the patterns established in other cases. In particular it offers further confirmation of the role played by child abuse in the formation of multiple personality, and of the link between multiple personality and artistic temperaments. The fact that its subject is male, with some 'female' personalities does give some revealing insights, worth setting against cases of female subjects with 'male' personalities.

Jeremy Hawthorn
University of Trondheim, Norway
February 1982

1
Multiple Personality

To talk of deviance is, of course, to imply that one is possessed of some concept of – or insight into – what is normal, and to consider multiple personality as a deviation from the norm forces us to consider what 'the norm' is. 'Personality' is, however, a very problematic concept, both in the specialized discourse of Psychology and also in everyday discussion. I think that it would be tedious to rehearse all the arguments that have taken place around the various attempts to define personality. I would, however, wish to venture a couple of preliminary assertions.

My first is that although personality may depend to some extent upon genetic factors, it is certainly influenced in its development by social pressures. Consequently, as society changes through history, changes in the nature of human personality can be detected – and literary works (as I shall argue) provide very good evidence of this. Secondly, I think that it is important to remember that our concern with cases of multiple personality should not lead us to suppose that the 'normal' personality is single and undivided in any absolute sense. A society experiencing civil war is clearly divided in a way that one enjoying comparative social concord is not, but this does not mean that the latter is possessed of neither tensions nor conflicts. One of the most authoritative studies of personality fragmentation, Ernest Hilgard's very comprehensive book *Divided Consciousness: Multiple Controls in Human Thought and Action* (1977) shows that the analogy with societies is not too far-fetched, for many of his studies of diversity and contradiction in human individuals relate to ostensibly 'normal' individuals, whose unity and integrity – like those of 'healthy' societies – often rest upon concealed processes of suppression and censorship.

It is time, however, to indicate in more detail what exactly is meant by multiple personality. For a person without medical or psychological training such as myself perhaps the most striking aspect of the phenomenon of multiple personality is the *sameness* of the case-histories that can be studied. For the lay investigator there is a tendency to assume that what we see as freaks of nature should be unique, unlike anything else. Yet the patterns that emerge in case-history after case-history of multiple personality are strikingly consistent. It seems to me that this consistency is, eventually, more noteworthy than the particular manifestations themselves. These last are extraordinary enough as it is, and this fact often leads those reporting

1

upon particular cases to concentrate much effort upon their description. By the time that one is reading one's fifth or sixth account, however, the particular details of the behaviour can be almost tiresomely familiar, and one craves information about the familial and social contexts in which the subject's multiplicity was formed. One reassuring aspect of this consistency is that as it continues through cases in which the subjects are clearly unaware of each others' existence then there seems little chance that we are dealing with a succession of good actors and actresses mimicking one anothers' symptoms.

To understand what multiple personality is we have to realize that a central component of it is the existence not just of contradictory behaviour patterns, but also of different and mutually exclusive memories. Thus we would be forced to conclude that neither St Paul nor a non-fictional version of Billy Liar suffered from multiple personality. The former, upon completing his journey to Damascus, may have got there as a different person, but he certainly knew what he had been before and how he changed. And Billy Liar, we assume, enjoys his fantasies so much precisely because he remembers what he is in his quotidian existence, and is aware of the contrast his imaginary life displays when set against his day-to-day self.

The individual suffering from a multiple-personality disorder, however, will have a memory barrier which separates off at least one of his or her personalities from one or more of the others. The dominant personality is likely to have a complete memory block concerning periods of time during which an alternative personality has been 'in control.' For this reason I find the following definition of multiple personality given by Taylor and Martin inadequate:

> A case of multiple personality we take to consist of two or more personalities each of which is so well developed and integrated as to have a relatively coordinated, rich, unified and stable life of its own. (Taylor and Martin 1944, 282)

On the basis of this definition we could say that a man whose behaviour at home was completely different from his behaviour at work, and for whom each separate behaviour complex was 'relatively coordinated, rich, unified and stable,' suffered from multiple personality. Multiple personality would indeed be a widespread phenomenon were this to be the case. I think that we must reject this definition and its implications, however, for even though the individual I have hypothesized may not be at all aware of the fact that his life can be seen as the combination of two separate behaviour-systems, he does have a memory which includes both. It is significant, however, that I have to draw attention to the inadequacy of the definition offered by Taylor and Martin, as it reminds us that *personality divisions* are widespread in our society and others, in people who cannot be categorized as suffering from multiple personality disorders. I will return to this point.

If memory division is a necessary, it is by no means a sufficient indication of multiple personality. The case reported by Charles L. Dana (Dana 1894), of a Mr S who, apparently as a result of a gas leak in his bedroom, suffered very considerable loss of memory – to the extent that he even had to learn to speak anew – falls shorts of what I would consider true multiple personality. Admittedly Mr S failed to recognize parents, sister or fiancée, had to learn to speak afresh, and picked up a German accent from his attendant in the course of so doing. And, in addition, when his memory returned after a period of three months he could remember nothing of the preceding three months. There are certainly two sets of experiences in one individual here which are separated by a memory block, but there is no indication that they manifested different personality traits. From what we can gather Mr S's behaviour during his 'missing' three months was consistent with his previous and subsequent personality.

Ernest Hilgard suggests that there are four main criteria of dissociated behaviour:

1   The dissociated systems can be identified as relatively coherent patterns of behavior with sufficient complexity to represent some degree of internal organization. [. . .]
2   There is commonly some amnesic barrier that prevents integration of the dissociated systems, at least during the time that the dissociation persists. This is the primary mark that distinguishes between alternating normal roles and alternating personalities as found in psychopathology. [. . .]
3   The experience of being 'possessed' by an alien personality represents a dissociation of a somewhat different kind, in which the mutual amnesias are not essential because the two 'personalities' in some sense conduct a battle for control of the one body. [. . .]
4   There are minor dissociations occurring in ordinary experience and in hypnosis that are so much less dramatic than fugues, multiple personalities, or possession states that they are more difficult to delimit precisely [. . .]. Among these are automatisms, such as compulsive behavior or obsessive thoughts, or the conversion reactions in hysteria.
(Hilgard 1977, 18)

This list suggests the somewhat paradoxical, but nevertheless important conclusions that multiple personality is both qualitatively different from 'normal' states but also resembles aspects of these states in a number of fascinating ways. My particular interest is with cases in which there exist both a memory block and radically different and contradictory personality manifestations. This is because, for reasons which I hope to make clear, I am interested in multiple personality as an apparent response to, or product of, conflict. The cases which I now wish to describe and discuss are all ones in which not only does an individual undergo major, extensive personality change – as manifested in behaviour, expressed beliefs and attitudes, and even appearance (many investigators are especially struck by this last aspect)

– but accompanying the distinction between alternative and contradictory personalities there is some memory block which renders at least one of the personalities ignorant of what has been done by one or more of the others. Thus the Sybil whose case is described in an account written by Flora Rheta Schreiber (1975) came to seek medical help unaware that her periods of blackout and memory loss were 'inhabited' by some 15 other personalities owning beliefs, attitudes and patterns of behaviour utterly foreign and, in some cases, morally repugnant to her. Typically, as Evelyn Lancaster points out (Lancaster and Poling 1958, 21), the original personality is unaware of ones that come later; and we can note in addition to this that where there is more than one additional personality each new one tends to be informed of the existence only of previously existing personalities. This pattern is significant because, as I shall argue, it helps to suggest a function that the emergence of new and separate personalities appears to perform.

An additional difficulty is that complicated states of what Morton Prince – a pioneer investigator of multiple personality – called 'co-consciousness', have frequently been revealed. Thus in Prince's classic study *The Dissociation of a Personality* (1906), we find that Sally, one of the dissociated personalities of the study's subject, Miss Beauchamp, claims to have been in existence since Miss Beauchamp's early childhood and to have 'observed' the life that Miss Beauchamp has lived. Sally, however, only started to enjoy periods of complete control (thus causing blackouts and times of memory loss for Miss Beauchamp) in Miss Beauchamp's early adulthood. Morton Prince reported that Sally had told him that she was aware of everything Miss Beauchamp said or did, and even of what she dreamed, as she herself never slept, so that even when she was not 'out' and in control she was in a sense co-conscious with the companion of the body they both inhabited, a companion who was unaware of her existence. Indeed, Prince goes further to offer substantiating evidence to suggest that Sally noticed things that the conscious Miss Beauchamp failed to observe, so that Sally could tell Prince where Miss Beauchamp had mislaid something in a fit of absent-mindedness.

A similar situation is reported upon by George B. Cutten in his account of John Kinsel (1903). In the final stage of Kinsel's second personality the apparently recent personality was able to reveal a comprehensive knowledge of Kinsel's earlier life, and, more strikingly, to recall details of this early life which Kinsel had forgotten about, but which independent checking revealed to be accurate. In a snippet of information which calls to mind aspects of the much later case of Sybil (Schreiber 1975) Cutten informs the reader that Kinsel, a theological student, had a particular problem with examinations as each of his two personalities could recall only that knowledge which had been acquired by that personality. Charles Dickens refers directly to this sort of experience in *Edwin Drood*:

As, in some cases of drunkenness, and in others of animal magnetism [*i.e. Mesmerism, or hypnotism, JH*], there are two states of consciousness which never clash, but each of which pursues its separate course as though it were continuous instead of broken (thus, if I hide my watch when I am drunk, I must be drunk again before I can remember where), so Miss Twinkleton has two distinct and separate phases of being. Every night, the moment the young ladies have retired to rest, does Miss Twinkleton smarten up her curls a little, brighten up her eyes a little, and become a sprightly Miss Twinkleton whom the young ladies have never seen. (Dickens 1982, 14)

We know from Fred Kaplan's *Dickens and mesmerism* (1975) that Dickens was well informed on such subjects, and it is noteworthy that the last sentence above was changed from 'a sprightlier Miss Twinkleton than the young ladies have ever seen', to emphasize the double personality.

In the late nineteenth-century *Dictionary of Psychological Medicine* edited by D. Hack Tuke, E. Azam gives an account of a certain Mlle R L, who, according to him, changed consciousness every evening at about eight o'clock. In her altered, evening state she spoke of herself in the third person, 'as children and Negroes do' according to Azam's commentary, and although aware of her 'daytime' state in her 'evening' consciousness, the reverse was not the case: during the day she had no apparent knowledge of what regularly happened to her at night (Tuke 1892, 400).

Joseph Breuer mentions a similar case in *Studies on Hysteria,* which he and Sigmund Freud co-wrote and published first in 1893 – the year before Tuke's account was published. Breuer's patient, Fräulein Anna O, was almost a mirror-image of Mlle R L, however. She experienced a

somnolent state in the afternoon, followed after sunset by the deep hypnosis for which she invented the technical name of 'clouds'. If during this she was able to narrate the hallucinations she had had in the course of the day, she would wake up clear in mind, calm and cheerful. She would sit down to work and write or draw far into the night quite rationally. At about four she would go to bed. Next day the whole series of events would be repeated. It was a truly remarkable contrast: in the day-time the irres-ponsible patient pursued by hallucinations, and at night the girl with her mind completely clear. (Freud and Breuer 1978, 80)

Ernest Hilgard, writing almost a century later, reports from studies on male alcoholics that they may face strikingly similar problems of memory retrieval, as what is forgotten in a state of sobriety may again be recalled when the subject is once more under the influence of alcohol (Hilgard 1977, 71). This seems to be a particular example of a more general phenomenon – clearly known to Dickens – which psychologists today term 'state-dependent learning'. Laboratory rats can be conditioned so that they are able to find their way along a maze only when under the influence of the drug they were affected by when first they learned the route. It seems likely that Dickens intended to use his knowledge of this curious process in *Edwin*

Drood – perhaps by having Jaspar murder (or attempt to murder) his victim while affected by opium, and then to forget about what he had done until the next time he was under the influence of the drug. One cannot help suspecting that the hair-parting Jaspar has in the middle of his head is meant to indicate that he is divided into two perhaps independent halves. I should perhaps add that I have no desire to indulge in the wild goose chase of trying to establish what the further development and ending of the unfinished plot of *Edwin Drood* were intended by Dickens to involve – if for no better reason than that I am not convinced that Dickens had necessarily made up his mind on this issue. Those who search the incomplete text for clues should remember that some of the completed works of Dickens contain, early on, highly misleading clues: Boffin's miserly thoughts in *Our Mutual Friend*, for example. What I am interested in is Dickens's fascination with such individual personality fragmentation, and his use of it to illustrate social and moral problems in his work.

Edwin Drood is much concerned with altered states of consciousness; it opens with the 'shattered consciousness' of a man awaking from an opium trance 'fantastically piec[ing] itself together.' But it is significant that Dickens relates such drug or hypnosis-induced fragmentation to a more familiar division: Miss Twinkleton is neither drug-addict nor alcoholic, but a supremely respectable school-teacher of young ladies whose alternating states are determined by the hours of work and relaxation. Such metaphorical and symbolic usages of the phenomenon of multiple personality to illuminate the everyday constitute an important contribution of literary works to our ability to understand the roots of personality fragmentation inside and outside the realms of literature.

To conclude my introductory remarks concerned with the difficulties involved in defining multiple personality, the schema of Henri Ellenberger's is worth referring to. Ellenberger suggests a tripartite classification: (1) simultaneous multiple personalities, (2) Successive multiple personalities, which can be further subdivided into (a) those mutually cognizant of each other, (b) those mutually amnesic, and (c) those in which one-way amenesia pertains, and (3) 'Personality clusters' (Ellenberger 1970, 131).

I would like at this stage to give a relatively detailed account of one case of multiple personality prior to moving to consider some of the significant similarities between a number of different examples of the same phenomenon. Morton Prince's study of Miss Beauchamp's case, to which I have already referred, is a classic account which, both in terms of subject and description, it is hard to better from more recent descriptions. The fact that Prince's account dates from the early twentieth century has also the advantage that it allows us to see the historical influences at work not just on the person investigated, but also on the person doing the investigating.

Miss Beauchamp was an American who came, typically, from an unhappy, middle-class family. The typicality of her class origin in accounts of multiple personality we may perhaps ascribe to the fact that the illnesses and disorders of the rich got studied more than those of the poor, except in the case of dangerously infectious diseases. The unhappiness of her home background seems more likely to have been a significant contributory factor in the emergence of her dissociation. According to Prince she

> was a nervous, impressionable child, given to day-dreaming and living in her imagination. Her mother exhibited a great dislike to her, and for no reason, apparently, excepting that the child resembled her father in looks. The general impression left on Miss Beauchamp's mind today is that of her presence having been ignored by her mother excepting on occasions of a reprimand. On the other hand, she herself idealized her mother, bestowing upon her almost morbid affection; and believing that the fault was her own, and that her mother's lack of affection was due to her own imperfections, and concluded that if she could only purify herself and make herself worthy, her mother's affection would be given her. The effect of all this upon the child was to suppress all disclosures of her mental life, and to make her morbidly reticent. She never gave expression to the ordinary feelings of everyday child life; never spoke to say that she was tired, hungry, or sleepy. She lived within herself and dreamed. (Prince 1906, 12)

Robert F. Jeans has suggested that

> the original personality in cases of multiple personality always encounters rejection at the hands of the mother or mother substitute. (Osgood *et al.* 1976, 271)

Mrs G, the subject of Robert Stoller's *Splitting* (1974), told him that her mother had wanted her to be a male, and dressed her like a boy. She had also told her daughter that she wished she had had little boys and that she never wanted a little girl. Not surprisingly Mrs G grew up with an extremely confused gender identity (Stoller 1974, 227).

Sally, the first of Miss Beauchamp's secondary personalities to appear (referred to as Chris by Prince early on in his account), claimed to Prince that she had come into existence – initially only as a co-conscious personality – at the time that Miss Beauchamp was learning to walk:

> [Sally] claimed to remember what she, as distinct from Miss Beauchamp, thought at the time when she was learning to walk. Then BI [Prince's term here for the primary personality] was frightened, she said, and wanted to go back, but subconscious Sally was not at all frightened and wanted to go ahead. (Prince 1906, 278)

If this account is to be believed (and it is easier to credit it after having noted similar crucial moments in other accounts) then it is significant that dissociation – even if of a partial or embryonic variety, as here – emerges in response to a traumatic social pressure which can be dealt with in two mutually exclusive ways. Mrs G's 'hidden voice', later to be named 'Charlie', emerged when she was four years old in apparent response to a similar situation. We can also note that, as Prince tells us, Miss Beauchamp's mother died when she was 13, an event which was so traumatic for her that it left her 'half delirious' for a number of weeks.

Apart from the presumed secret existence of Sally as a co-consciousness, Miss Beauchamp developed in an outwardly normal way until her young adulthood, when another deeply disturbing event took place for her. During this time she was a student at a hospital, and one appropriately dramatic night, when not only was there a violent storm raging outside but she had been terrified by a deranged patient rushing towards her, she caught sight of a young man in whom she had a romantic interest at the window of a room in the Nurses' Home in which she was living. She managed to meet this 'William Jones' at the door of the Home without arousing the suspicions of the other nurses, and at the door an 'exciting scene' took place in which Mr Jones apparently used extremely passionate language to her. After this 'psychical catastrophe', as Prince describes it, Miss Beauchamp suffered from retrograde amnesia which removed all knowledge of the event, and for the next six years she alternated with a different, new personality. Finally, another psychic shock reminiscent of the first (she received a letter from Jones using language similar to that used at the door of the Nurses' Home, which she read during a violent storm) induced the birth of an additional personality based on her self prior to the first catastrophe.

When Prince first met her he described the three personalities he managed to isolate as, 'The Saint, The Woman, and The Devil', which tells us a lot about Prince as well as about Miss Beauchamp. These three personalities were, after a while, immediately recognizable to him; their appearance was different, and their general behaviour gave them away before they actually said anything. (This phenomenon is stressed by many writers on the subject of multiple personality, particularly Schreiber [1975] and Thigpen and Cleckley [1954, 1957]. It is interesting to note that very often when a male investigator is describing the difference between two personalities of a woman, one will be described as clearly 'prettier', which gives food for thought concerning the extent to which sexual attractiveness is exclusively physical).

Prince eventually found more personalities, and he labelled them as BI, BII, BIII and BIV. His methods of categorization are complex, and change during the book, so that it is easy to get confused about these separate personalities, but it is significant that Chris/Sally is additional to the above, as Prince never really accepted her as a proper personality – of which more later. BII emerged only under hypnosis.

Many of the most interesting parts of Prince's account consist of statements from Chris/Sally (Sally hereafter), who told Prince of the difference between her and Miss Beauchamp's dominant personality:

'She does not enjoy wickedness. I do. She thinks she is going to be a [*religious JH*] sister. She won't as long as I am here.'

'Why?'

(With an expression of disgust on her face.) 'I have a great objection to having nothing to eat, and doing things I am told to do, and going to church and being preached at. I have other things to do.'

'What?'

(Laughing.) 'To smoke cigarettes.' (Prince 1906, 56)

Miss Beauchamp did not smoke, and could not understand the objectionable taste she found in her mouth after Sally had been smoking (just as Eve White could not understand the hangovers left for her to suffer by the drinking of her body's other personality – Eve Black [Thigpen and Cleckley 1957, 82, etc]). Miss Beauchamp and Sally differed in many other ways; the former was terrified of spiders, whilst the latter was not bothered by them, and even left a box containing spiders for Miss Beauchamp to discover, open and be terrified by.

Sally admitted to Prince that she was jealous of Miss Beauchamp and that she hated her, and in a sequence like something out of a French farce, would unravel a piece of worsted work as fast as Miss Beauchamp was able to make it. BIV paid Sally back, however, by repeatedly destroying the auto-biography which Sally later tried to write. As Prince puts it, in another revealing comment,

> Harmony was about as stable as that of the South American Republics, of which one is constantly reminded by the repeated revolutionary out-breaks against the psychic autonomy of Miss Beauchamp. (Prince 1906, 428)

One of the most significant details in Prince's account (bearing in mind the nature of the psychic shock that appears to have been decisive in the adult experience of dissociation) is that, as Miss Beauchamp told Prince,

> what particularly distressed her was the fact that since that eventful night she had tried to break with the past, while Sally, [*of whose existence Miss Beauchamp is now aware, JH*] by corresponding and making engagements [*with Jones, JH*], and thereby breaking the promises that BI made, was constantly putting her in false positions. (Prince 1906, 222)

On one occasion, indeed, Sally wrote to Jones asking him to come and take her away. According to Sally herself,

> [Jones] sent a great, great many letters to tell C [*Miss Beauchamp; Prince has changed his nomenclature again! JH*] how sorry he was, but she wouldn't open any of them, even when they were directed in different handwriting. She sent them all back at first, afterward she dropped them in the fire, and I was simply aching to read them. Not because I cared particularly about J[ones]; I didn't, but neither did I care about C, and

of the two he was certainly much the more interesting [. . .]. (Prince 1906, 390)

Sally's exuberant, unrepressed, apparently amoral attitudes and behaviour are typical of secondary personalities in many cases of dissociation. C.E. Cory suggests that his subject's secondary personality 'B', 'in common with cases of this type,'

> manifests an extreme egoism. She is never genuinely interested in anything that does not bear upon her own welfare. The conversation must be centered about her, her past, present, or future. She is utterly incapable of a truly unselfish thought or act. (Cory 1920, 288)

Evelyn Lancaster's secondary personality Eve Black conforms to this pattern, and appears not only to have gone through an illegal marriage ceremony with a highly dubious character – an event of which her dominant personality remained in blissful ignorance – but also to have slept with the husband her dominant personality was trying to get rid of because he disgusted her. And this act was committed merely in order to obtain some new dresses!

In the case of Miss Beauchamp and others, however, the relationships between her different personalities were not completely antagonistic and destructive. Sally appears to have saved Miss Beauchamp (and, of course, herself) from a suicide attempt, just as, many years later, Sybil was to be prevented from self-destruction by one of her other selves.

Attempting to gather the foregoing into certain general points it is possible to draw up a list of the 'family resemblances' (and 'family' is a particularly appropriate word) shared by a number of the best-documented cases of multiple personality. So far as B.C.A. (B.C.A. 1908), Eve (Lancaster and Poling 1958; Thigpen and Cleckley 1954, 1957) and Sybil (Schreiber 1975) are concerned, we can indicate a striking correlation. All of the following elements seem to have been operative in these (and other) cases: (1) the subject (who, in about two-thirds of the reported cases will be a woman), has been a nervous, introverted and imaginative child, often highly responsive to aesthetic or artistic stimuli from, for instance, films or novels; (2) he or she will have had some sort of traumatic shock in early childhood, often associated with a parent or close relative's death, or with sexual molestation from an adult; (3) much later in life, usually in late adolescence or early adulthood, some form of tension or conflict which the subject is unable to resolve because of the existence of taboos or repressions will emerge to torture him or her; (4) in almost every case the existence of strong – usually extreme – religious belief on the part of the subject or the subject's family will be a significant factor in the tensions mentioned above, and (5) whether the multiple personalities emerge in one stage or in a number of stages the new, emergent personality will be free of the taboo or repression and thus able to ignore or solve the major tension or conflict (although only for him or herself, and not for the original personality).

Ralph B. Allison (1974), in his ironically titled short article 'A Guide to Parents: how to Raise your Daughter to have Multiple Personalities', lists seven 'rules' for producing a (female) dissociated personality on the basis of a number of cases studied. These conform to a large extent to my five points above, although Allison omits mention of the near-omnipresence of a religious element in the family background. His 'ideal' parents should not want their child in the first place, should create a polarity between mother and father for the child, should make sure that a parent (especially a favoured one) disappears before the child is six, should encourage sibling rivalry, should be ashamed of their family tree, should see to it that their daughter's first sexual experience is traumatic and that she cannot tell them about it, and, finally and perhaps more controversially, they should make her home life so miserable that she wants to escape from it, but should then ensure that she marries 'a sexual deviate who can carry on in your tradition'.

My own feeling is that although generalizations are dangerous, and although different cases of multiple personality may well have different physiological and organic causal elements, let alone social and familial ones, there do seem to be two crucial components in the chain of circumstances that produces a multiple personality. Firstly, a child must have, early on in life, developed some sort of predisposition to dissociation in response to an unbearable traumatic shock or pressure; secondly, the individual must, later on in life, be caught in some sort of double-bind in which situation anything he or she does will produce what appear to be unacceptable results.

To fill out the reader's picture I would like, at this point, to work through my five main points and to give substantiating evidence in the form of details from case histories from a wide range of historical periods and societies.

1   *The subject's nervous and imaginative disposition.* Ernest Hilgard (1977) points out that imaginative activity already involves a form of dissociation, as the constraints of ordinary reality are set aside during it. In a study by Hilgard's wife, Josephine Hilgard, it was found that

> the trait above all others that characterized hypnotic susceptibility was the capacity for [. . .] imaginative involvement. Typical areas of involvement were reading, especially fiction, including science fiction; the dramatic arts, acting, watching, and informal dramatization; religion of personal commitment; affective arousal through sensory stimulation; adventuresomeness as in 'physical' spatial experiences such as mountain climbing, cave exploring, or skin diving, or a 'mental' adventuresomeness in experimenting with drugs, parapsychology, or oriental beliefs.
> (Hilgard 1977, 104)

This would suggest that susceptibility to being hypnotized – in the broadest sense a form of predisposition to a type of personality dissociation – has something in common with a vulnerability to the experience of multiple personality disorders. Nearly all of the case-histories of those who have suffered from such disorders reveal that the subjects in question were 'imaginative' in some way or other from childhood onwards. Thus Sybil (Schreiber 1975) was a child with very considerable artistic talents – painting, playing the guitar, and so on – and some of her later, separate selves retained and developed these abilities. I.M. Allen tells us of Gwen Y, the subject of his investigation, that she 'had always been a nervous girl, read a great deal and was particularly fond of Hardy' (Allen 1932, 321). In B.C.A.'s account of herself she notes early on that she is 'sensitive and responsive to impressions', and that at the theatre she loses herself in the play and feels keenly all the emotions portrayed by the actors (B.C.A. 1908, 242). Breuer's account of Anna O starts with the information that she had great poetic and imaginative gifts, although these were under the control of a sharp and critical common sense. He adds that one of her essential character traits was 'sympathetic kindness' (Freud and Breuer 1978, 73).

The ability to enter into an artistic performance is perhaps most strikingly exhibited by Jack Poulting/Poultney, the subject of S.I. Franz's book *Persons One and Three* (1933). Attending his first-ever sound film along with other First World War veterans who had been invited by the management of the cinema to see a performance of the film *All Quiet on the Western Front*, Jack's response to the film indicated a total suspension of disbelief on his part:

> When the noise of the bombardment or barrage had been in progress for only a few seconds, he rose from his seat, called to his companions to take cover, ran down the aisle of the theater towards the stage, and then he dived into the orchestra pit. He kept calling to his fellow soldiers to take cover, and to get ready to repel an expected attack. (Franz 1933, 146)

Cornelius C. Wholey, in his 'A Case of Multiple Personality,' specifically compares his subject Mrs X with Morton Prince's Miss Beauchamp:

> Both girls, as children, were manifestly neurotic; in each case there is a history of 'fainting' spells in childhood; of sleepwalking, or somnambu-listic episodes; of attempts to 'run away.' Neither was able to pursue a given task for any length of time. Both were day-dreamers; both came into conflict with one or the other parent. (Wholey 1933, 657)

He notes in addition that after her childhood Mrs X

> developed a passion for the movies, and would get excited over them; could relate the scenes in detail. She read many light novels, would read in bed all through the night. She would get excited over the love stories, and tell them over and over. She was constantly romancing. (This emotional response is interesting in view of the fact that later as her split-off personality developed she would emerge as different imaginary characters. Evidently she identified herself with various characters she

had encountered in the movies and in fiction. For instance, at one time she became 'Lucille', a Chicago cabaret girl who could toe dance. Again she emerged in a split-off state as a 'society girl', relating while in this personality, that a wealthy man whom she had refused to marry had kidnapped her, and put her in a house of prostitution. Again she was a 'New York woman' who was married, but had a secret lover. In her early romancing over stories and movies she was laying the foundation for her later identification, in split-off states, with her fictional heroines.) (Wholey 1933, 658)

I quote this passage at length because if it is the case that a susceptibility to fictional representations can be established as in some way similar to or involved in the finding of solutions to problems via personality dissociation, then discovering the function that personality dissociation performs may give us some hint of some of the functions that imaginative engagement with fiction can in turn perform. I put this point forward in full awareness of the dangers of seeking for mechanical or simplistic parallels here, and I should stress that there is clearly much that the writing and reading of imaginative literature – for instance – does that is quite different from what is gained from personality dissociation. Nevertheless, Wholey's comments suggest that if we were to look into the usefulness of, say, pulp romantic fiction to its readers, we might find that it allowed for a controlled and socially acceptable solution to pressures and tensions within the family and society at large that has something in common with the relief dissociation provides for those with multiple personality disorders. It is certainly the case that the literate have forms of imaginative escape and 'doubling' available to them which are denied to the illiterate, and I will expand upon this point later on.

2 *Childhood trauma.* The trauma involved can take various forms, but usually it seems to be associated with the death or loss of a parent or parent-substitute, or sexual molestation. Sybil's schizophrenic mother subjected her to repeated physical torture which had strong sexual overtones, and on top of this the death of her grandmother – an important source of love and protection for her – increased her sense of isolation and oppression. The death of her grandmother was also of crucial significance to Evelyn Lancaster and this was accentuated by her mother's insistence that she kiss the corpse of the departed in the coffin prior to its burial. I.M. Allen gives an account of the childhood of his subject – Gwen Y – which includes a familiar pattern:

Gwen Y was one of a family of six in moderate circumstances. She was five years old when her mother died and was allowed to see her mother after death. She and the other children were sent to a school, but, when their father deserted them shortly afterwards, they were transferred to a workhouse. Gwen Y was much upset at being separated from her younger brother, then an infant, and dreamed about him for many years.

[. . .] When she left [school] she was told to be very careful as her mother
was as good as in Hell. (Allen 1932, 320)

Allen notes, later on in his account, that when Gwen Y was taken to see her
mother's body she screamed and ran away.

Henry Herbert Goddard (1927) reports of his subject, Norma, that her
identical twin died at the age of 10 from diphtheria, and that this was
followed by a succession of other traumatic shocks as her childhood
unfolded. She was frightened by the onset of puberty, her parents and other
siblings died, and she was treated cruelly by an aunt who looked after her.
Her aunt forced her to sleep upstairs in spite of her expressed fear of the
dark, and as she went upstairs to bed her aunt would call out to her and
suggest that something was about to leap upon her. A dark comment of
Goddard's also makes reference to Norma's striking of him and calling upon
her (dead) mother to 'protect her against daddy' (1927, 123).

This may not refer to any specific ill-treatment, but it is the case that
sexual molestation by a parent seems to be a common experience of those
who later dissociate or hallucinate. Some of the accounts given of such early
sexual assaults are horrifying. Ernest Hilgard gives details of a particularly
unpleasant recent case, involving a subject Katherine/Kathy: Kathy

[. . .] reported an attempt by a younger brother to have sex with her at the
age of 5, at the urging of an older sister, but he was unsuccessful and she
did not know what it was all about. The important incident occurred at
the age of 7, when an older brother forced both oral and anal sex on her in
a corn field near their home. This was a painful and frightening experience for her. She could not explain why she was late for dinner, and when
her father punished her severely for being late, she accepted this as
punishment also for her sexual transgression. Katherine, who does not
recall the incident, remembers a frightening dream a year later, 'A wolf
came out of a corn field, I ran inside to lock the windows, but the wolf
jumped in.' The split in personality is dated from this event. [. . .]

The unfortunate experiences with sex did not stop with this incident.
At the age of 10 she saw her 12-year-old sister raped by several boys; at the
age of 17 she was raped by three boys, and on another occasion her father,
while drunk, made sexual advances to her, but Kathy [*the secondary personality, JH*] emerged to stop him [. . .]. (Hilgard 1977, 35)

If this seems like an extreme case, the catalogue of similar experiences
suffered by a number of subjects detailed by Ralph B. Allison suggests,
unfortunately, that perhaps it is not.

Elizabeth was raped on the school grounds at age 11. Because of her
mother's tirades against her aunt's sexual behavior, Elizabeth didn't dare
tell her for fear of being branded immoral and evil.
Kay was sexually assaulted at age 13 by a band of Hells Angels while
living at grandmother's ranch. [. . .]

Doris's stepfather refused to let her go to school past the sixth grade because boys were in the school. He constantly accused her of sexual misconduct of which she was too shy to be guilty. This engendered the same guilty feeling about sexuality as the episodes in the lives of the other two girls. (Allison 1974, 85)

The case history of Mrs G conforms to the same pattern. Robert Stoller sums up the history of her early sexual mistreatment, advancing a rather dubious explanation of it at the same time:

Mrs G not only wanted to be against her mother's body: she also craved her father. This must have been why she was, in fact, so often the victim of infamous assaults by men. A grandfather, two uncles, and several strangers had already had intercourse with her by the time she was eight; and without letup thereafter, boys, adolescents, adults, and aging men found her sexually compliant. (Stoller 1974, 278)

Stoller elsewhere reveals that at the age of ten Mrs G had been the victim of anal rape, which hardly suggests quite the compliance argued for above.

Doris Gruenewald (1971) reports that her subject's secondary personality B came into existence as an imaginary playmate in her sixth year after verified sexual molestation by her stepfather, which continued for several years. And Morton Schatzman's *The Story of Ruth* (1980), while it is concerned with a hallucinating rather than a dissociating personality, reports repeated sexual attacks on her from her father. It is worth noting, too, that Sylvia Plath (again, not an example of dissociation, but someone who suffered a schizophrenic breakdown and had – as I will go on to argue – a particular interest in personality division) was traumatically affected by the birth of her brother and the death of her father.

Henri F. Ellenberger (1970) quotes a particularly interesting account of an Italian girl, Elena, who spoke only French in her periods of dissociation although she thought that she was speaking Italian. She finally remembered having been the victim of her father's incestuous attacks which included attempts to put his tongue in her mouth. Ellenberger notes that her dissociation was thus an attempt to repress the memory of her father's 'tongue' (language), and of his assaults upon her.

All of these traumatic experiences gave those who experienced them splendid reasons for wishing to be someone else in contexts where they could not be someone else. This form of entrapment seems the classic basis for dissociation: if you cannot solve your problems by being one person, you become two. The sexual element is also important for an understanding of the continuation of the double-bind into adulthood: the child cannot be another person because he or she has no power to change his or her social role; the adult has no power to change or ignore his or her sexuality – a sexuality which may have highly undesirable or unwanted social repercussions. And if the childhood solution to unbearable problems resulting from *other people's* sexuality has been that of dissociation, then the later, adult solution to problems resulting from *one's own* sexuality may be the same. This suggests that a mechanism of early conditioning leading to a later predisposition to solve problems by means of dissociation may be at work – a suggestion made by Breuer in *Studies on Hysteria*:

> I suspect that the duplication of psychical functioning, whether this is habitual or caused by emotional situations in life, acts as a substantial *predisposition* to a genuine pathological splitting of the mind. (Freud and Breuer 1978, 314)

At this stage of my argument I should perhaps make it clear that I do not intend to argue that the literary works at which I will be looking in the latter part of this book will all reveal evidence of such clinical conditioning. But people can be predisposed to behave in certain ways without their being clinically conditioned, and it is very striking that many of the works I shall be looking at specifically relate childhood experiences to adult 'split' behaviour. Marlow in *She Stoops to Conquer* explains his differential behaviour to women of upper and lower-class origins by reference to his upbringing; Charlotte Brontë details the existence of childhood repression in the case of both Lucy Snowe and little Polly in *Villette*; the obsessive behaviour of Henry Sutpen in Faulkner's *Absalom, Absalom!* is seen to stem from a traumatic childhood slight; Jean Rhys's 'Rochester' in *Wide Sargasso Sea* tells the reader that he learned to suppress his emotions as a child; and although the hero and heroine of, respectively, Dickens's *Great Expectations* and Sylvia Plath's *The Bell Jar* are not exactly depicted as having been traumatized in their youth, their adult lives clearly seem to involve some 'living out' of much earlier tensions.

3 *Adult trauma or double-bind as triggering element in the later dissociation.* S.I. Franz, in his account of Jack Poulting/Poultney in *Persons One and Three* (1933) remarks that

> every change which had been observed, or of which we have had reasonable information, was known to be preceded by a period in which he was under what is commonly called 'emotional strain.' (Franz 1933, 188)

These 'strains' included serious financial problems, leaving America for Britain to volunteer to fight in the First World War, visiting his native Ireland very briefly and seeing his family, being punished for smoking on a British troopship by being suspended by the thumbs and, it is presumed, the experience of war, seeing friends killed, and being captured. The triggering event which released his suppressed, original personality was seeing the African town Voi on a map: while in Voi he had seen a pet monkey, which he had tethered, devoured by a tiger while he took refuge up a tree. Ellenberger (1970) has suggested that the monkey incident was important to him in this way because into it he displaced previous emotions experienced when, in a similar situation, a companion of his had been eaten by a marauding animal. Whether or not we accept this hypothesis it seems clear that some sort of retrospective double-bind was the result of an inability to reconcile his guilt at the death and his relief concerning his own escape.

It is interesting, I think, that Franz's account suggests that his subject responded to pressures emanating from a less confined social sphere than appeared to be the case with many of the female subjects whose experiences we have looked at. We will see this pattern repeated later on when the case of Silas Pronge is briefly discussed. War, unemployment, financial crisis: these seem to be the sources of personality dissociation for men rather than complex and contradictory personal relationships and sexual experiences. Again, this differentiation can be seen too in the literary works we will examine later on. For Golyadkin in *The Double*, Pip in *Great Expectations*, Willy Loman in *Death of a Salesman* and the unnamed narrator of *The Secret Sharer* their problems stem, typically, from the world of work, money and public life. Lucy Snowe in *Villette*, and Esther Greenwood in *The Bell Jar* experience problems which are related to the *lack* of a public, working life, and it is significant that when Lucy Snowe achieves this she overcomes her emotional difficulties. I am not suggesting that women without jobs do not work, by the way; nor am I suggesting that personal relationships and sexuality are unconnected with public and social pressures. Indeed, the 'personal problems' experienced by many women are problems precisely because they are made so by the operation of social taboos and conventions.

A classic example of this can be found in Thigpen and Cleckley's account of Evelyn Lancaster's dissociation in their book *The Three Faces of Eve*.

> Six years ago she had married a young man. He was a faithful and serious member of the Catholic Church. As a Baptist, serious too in her own religion, she had had misgivings about the oath she was required to take, an oath promising that her children would be carefully brought up as Catholics. Despite these misgivings she had so committed herself and had intended to carry out the solemn agreement.
>
> At the first interview [*with the doctor, JH*] she admitted that she could not bring herself to send her little girl, Bonnie, to her husband's church [. . .]. (Thigpen and Cleckley 1957, 8)

The situation in which Eve finds herself, then, represents a classic example of the double-bind. If she follows the requirements of her religion she will break a promise, (forbidden by her religion!), and if she does what her promise binds her to do she will offend her religious principles. In this situation we can see, I think, a pattern similar to that found in Morton Prince's account of Miss Beauchamp's entrapment between the rival demands of her sexuality and social convention. Prince, in fact, gives details of one of Miss Beauchamp's dreams the symbolism of which seems pretty transparent to a post-Freudian reader. Miss Beauchamp dreamed that she was in a coffin lined with hands,

But the pillow moved – long freably worms wriggled out of it, covering her from head to foot, and she screamed with terror. When she tried to escape the worms, the hands clutched her. When she would avoid the hands, the worms went through and through her. (Prince 1906, 338)

Prince adds that the dream also involved some earlier 'Egyptian mummy' images, which suggests that a fear of pregnancy might be at work in the dream machinery somewhere.

I have suggested a tension between sexuality and social convention in Miss Beauchamp's dissociative behaviour; had she merely responded in disgust to Jones's advances then the experience of his intemperate language might well have presented her with no problems. But the continued interest in him of Sally, her asocial personality, suggests strongly that Miss Beauchamp was split between being sexually excited by and attracted to Jones, and unable to square her insistent sexuality with social convention and taboo. Prince does not make this hypothesis, and his attitude towards the Sally personality suggests the operation of some form of sexual censorship in his own analysis of the case. Thus it is noteworthy that whereas at the start of his account he suggests that

Cases of this kind are commonly known as 'double' or 'multiple personality', according to the number of persons represented, but a more correct term is *disintegrated* personality, for each secondary personality is a part only of a normal whole self. (Prince 1906, 3)

when he later starts to talk of finding Miss Beauchamp's 'real self' amongst the contending personalities he is, implicitly, abandoning this schema. It is as if he cannot bring himself to admit that what Sally stands for is a disintegrated part of a 'normal' young woman. I think that this point is important because it suggests that the larger tensions and contradictions existing in society at large can enter into the the individual's life and experience at several levels – not least through the mediation of the medical profession.

Here again the evidence of the literary works I will look at in detail later on bears out this impression. The long discussion between Golyadkin and his doctor at the start of *The Double*, for example, concentrates to a striking extent upon the former's *social* rather than medical problems, and the doctor's response to their presentation seems to be at least in part responsible for Golyadkin's accelerating collapse from this point of the novel onwards. Lucy Snowe's relations with the medical profession are of course especially complex as her doctor is also the man to whom she is sexually attracted in the first half of the novel. And for Esther Greenwood in *The Bell Jar* her medical student boyfriend Buddy Willard, and the doctor who treats her for her depression – Doctor Gordon – both form complex aspects of her problem rather than of its solution.

As I will go on to discuss later, many investigators into multiple personality suggest that the causal factors can be limited to the subject's intimate personal relationships — especially within the family. My own feeling is that family relationships, like one's relationship with a medical practitioner, are not just personal relationships; they involve and are constituted by larger social and historical assumptions, tensions, and so on. How difficult it would be to separate the 'personal' from the 'social' in Miss Beauchamp's case! We see this more clearly, of course, because looking at a case in the past we are more aware of the historically changing nature of personal relationships. One of the illuminating aspects of studying literary accounts of dissociation and breakdown is that it highlights such historically and socially transitory elements in personal and familial relationships.

In his search for Miss Beauchamp's 'real self' Morton Prince seems to adopt a sort of legalistic view of the matter, as if ownership could be determined by original occupancy:

> Sally, whoever she might be, was clearly not the original Miss Beauchamp, and not a normal person. (Prince 1906, 234)

Had Prince pursued the logic of his term 'disintegrated personality' he would surely have seen that Sally could be a component part of a normal person without being, herself, a fully normal individual. But the earlier implications of the concept of disintegration are abandoned in favour of a search for an original Miss Beauchamp whose identity excluded such aspects as were represented by Sally. It is perhaps a matter of history — and Freud — that one hardly needs to explain why, by 1920, C.E. Cory in his article 'A Divided Self' is able to note confidently that 'the sex impulse was a strong factor in the dissociation' (Cory 1920, 285). Although, as Cory says, the immediate cause of dissociation for his subject A/B was the shock received from the tragic death of her father, which precipitated a lack of coordination so grave that for a while she was hardly able to walk, the impulse of sexuality seems somehow to be centrally involved in the split, as the nature of the two personalities suggests. As Cory writes,

> I have said that the sexual instinct is at the center of the group of associations that constitute B. A says that she thinks of nothing else. That is not quite true, for she is interested in her singing. But sex is never far in the background, and the deeper down you go into her subconsciousness the clearer it becomes that A is not far wrong. A's early training both at home and at the convent, was one of repression, one that put a strict taboo upon all reference to sexual matters. The result upon A's, at the time, highly sexual nature was to isolate this desire, and drive it underground. (Cory 1929, 289)

Sex and religion together form a peculiarly potent combination, creating not only conflicting and irreconcilable desires and wishes, but both seemingly immovable and intransigent in their demands. Evelyn Lancaster's case illustrates perfectly how powerful religious taboos can be. She is caught between her promise and the requirements of her religion, and no meta-belief can mediate between the two. It is, incidentally, a tantalizing aspect of Prince's *The Dissociation of a Personality* that he refers obliquely to a promise made by Miss Beauchamp to her former preceptor not to reveal certain things to anyone; one cannot help wondering whether this promise double-bound her in the way in which Evelyn Lancaster's did.

B.C.A. is relatively imprecise concerning the immediate triggering cause of her mature dissociation, but what she does tell the reader suggests that it was something comparable to the problems faced by Miss Beauchamp and Evelyn Lancaster. In her case we again find the classic two stages: early shock followed by childish rebellion or breakdown, followed a couple of decades later by a similar pattern:

> A year previous to this division of personality a long nervous strain, covering a period of four years, had culminated in the death of one very dear to me. (B.C.A. 1908, 242)

In the case of Gwen Y, I.M. Allen gives more detailed information, and this is sufficient to confirm that the adult triggering cause was a particularly intolerable domestic situation. She lived in a household with a Mr and Mrs Z, and for 18 months prior to the onset of her dissociative illness Mrs Z had been making sexual advances to her while at the same time having an affair with a lodger.

4 *Religious belief as a contributory factor.* Clearly this aspect of the creation of multiple personality disorders is of a different category from my earlier points, and is I suspect far more culture-specific. The important thing about an atmosphere of (normally extreme, fundamentalist) religious belief is that it taboos certain possible solutions to problems faced by the subjects in their adult lives. I would expect that any strongly held, socially reinforced 'total' belief system could, in the right circumstances, perform the same role. Whatever the truth of the matter, it is an undeniable fact that, reading through different case-histories, it is almost impossible to find examples where *no* mention of religious belief on the part of the subject, his or her family or community is made. I have already referred to Miss Beauchamp's desire to become a nun, and to the centrality of religious tensions to Evelyn Lancaster's pre-dissociative problems. Of course, some allowance needs to be made for the fact that many of the reports with which we are concerned date from periods of more widespread and more intense religious commitment, and we must also remember that those suffering mental strain or breakdown are more likely to seek the consolations of religion – or to encourage others to seek it for them. Nevertheless, even after such due allowance has been made, the insistent recurrence of the religious element in cases of multiple personality is very striking. In one of the very earliest accounts of a relatively mild dissociation on the part of a 16-year-old Scottish

servant girl (II. Dewar 1823), the subject, who according to Dewar was on the verge of puberty,

> fell asleep [*in a manner already described, JH*], imagined herself an Episcopal clergyman, went through the ceremony of baptizing three children, and gave an appropriate *extempore* prayer (Dewar 1823, 366)

If this last example does no more than suggest the greater predominance of religious belief in the Scotland of the early nineteenth century from the Britain of today, the case of Silas Pronge, reported on by a number of commentators, indicates that the repressions and taboos associated with religious belief were a dominant factor in the dissociation. As I mentioned when talking of the case of Jack Poulting/Poultney, the cases of Pronge and Poulting/Poultney reveal a much more significant element of pressure on the individual coming directly from outside the family, and the fact that both are male indicates that the sorts of pressure on men and women are likely to be rather different. But more of this later. Robert Howland Chase (1918), one of the later commentators upon Pronge's story, gives interesting details of an episode in Pronge's life that occurred at about the age of 30, some 30 years before his dissociation: at this time he

> experienced a pronounced crisis, which was interpreted by himself and friends as a visitation of Providence. After this attack suddenly his character and mode of life completely changed from that of an acknowledged atheist to that of a devoted Christian worker. It was thus related of him: 'One day, while walking in the open country he perceived a voice speaking to him. It said, "Go to the Chapel! Go to the Chapel!" "To what chapel," he inquired of his invisible monitor. "To the Christian Chapel," was the reply.' (Chase 1918, 152)

The details thus given were apparently adequate, for Pronge became an itinerant preacher for 25 years, and subsequently retired to become a carpenter again. But after marriage to his second wife he discovered that she disapproved of his long absences from home, and thus confined his occasional preaching to the near vicinity (Hodgson 1891, 228). As a result of this, Richard Hodgson reports his testifying,

> he became somewhat troubled, thinking that he was not so active in his religious work as he should be. This thought that he was not 'on the path of duty' weighed on his mind, and he seems inclined to think that if he had been in active religious service, and therefore contented with his work, the experiences which he subsequently underwent would never have occurred. (Hodgson 1891, 228)

He disappeared from home after having drawn out all his money, and was found in a strange town keeping a store and believing himself to be an 'A.J. Brown'. Investigations into his experiences, in which William James among others participated, revealed that his two personalities were each ignorant of the other, but that fundamentalist religious belief was common to both of them.

Charles E. Cory (1919), writing about the authoress Patience Worth, who in her non-literary life was a Mrs John Curran, revealed that

> the thing that interests [Patience Worth] most is not her own personality, but the religious and spiritual truth that she presents in her poetry and fiction. (Cory 1919, 406)

Her literary works, appparently produced through 'automatic writing', were believed by Mrs Curran to be the compositions of a long-dead person using the medium of her body as a means of communication, and while writing she appeared to be experiencing a form of dissociation. Cory suggests that the novels, plays and poems so produced were of high artistic merit, but her claim to quantitative achievement seems less likely to be disputed than that to qualitative merit; at the time Cory was writing she had it seems written some 1500 poems.

John Kinsel, whose case is reported on in an article by George B. Cutten (1903), not only came from a family riddled with alcoholism and insanity, but the particular form of insanity suffered from by his maternal aunt took the form of refusing to see anyone or do anything, with the sole exception of reading the bible. Kinsel himself was chosen by his family to study for the ministry although he felt no particular religious vocation.

A similar atmosphere of heavy and oppressive fundamentalism seems to have surrounded the life of Mollie Fancher, whose case Abram H. Dailey discusses in the revealingly titled *Mollie Fancher, The Brooklyn Enigma: An Authentic Statement of Facts in the Life of Mary J. Fancher, the Psychological Marvel of the Nineteenth Century* (1894). One brief detail (shorter, in fact, than the title of the book) from this rather tedious account should suffice. Miss Fancher's dissociative problems stemmed from an accident almost identical to that which led to dissociation for Pirandello's 'Henry IV' character: she fell off her horse. Immediately after this, her life was feared for, and in the intervals between the doctor's questions to her, Dailey informs us that her friends gathered round her and 'sang a favorite hymn with low, sad voices, "Nearer My God to Thee"' (Dailey 1894, 19). She got nearer very slowly, however, living about as long in her changed state as we presume Pirandello's character did in his.

In another celebrated – and much-reported upon – early case, that of Mary Reynolds, investigations revealed that not only were her parents both very pious and intelligent, 'in sentiment Baptists' (Plumer 1860, 811), but that the only knowledge shared equally by her two personalities was a familiarity with the scriptures. By this time the reader should not be surprised to learn that in their account of the Revd Thomas Hanna's case, Boris Sidis and Simon P. Goodhart report that Hanna's religious feelings developed early on, and that 'The change from an architectural to a theological field of work seemed to have come about not without an intense struggle for the young man' (Sidis and Goodhart 1905, 130). But even the by now well prepared reader might be somewhat taken aback by the nature of the religious element in the case of the Mrs X described by Cornelius C. Wholey (1933). Whenever she had a dissociative fit her neighbours, who took care of her, sprinkled holy water on her and called upon the Father, Son and Holy Ghost to 'go to'. Such injunctions notwithstanding, Mrs X's return to comparative normality seems only to have followed a change of domestic environment.

In the case of Sybil (Schreiber 1975), the home-town setting, although that of a mid-twentieth-century American community, seems to have provided a similar atmosphere of repressive religious belief:

> Willow Corners [*the home town, JH*], as any sociologist could predict, had churches of many faiths. The fundamentalist groups ranged from the Seventh-Day Baptists, who had founded the town's first church, to the Seventh-Day Adventists, the Church of Saint John Baptist de la Salle, and the Church of the Assembly of God. The Methodists, Congregationalists and Lutherans all looked askance at one another and at the Roman Catholics, whom they regarded as the incarnation of evil.
>
> Bigotry was rampant, and the town, although self-righteous in its utterances, was often cruel in its behaviour. There were jeers for the mentally retarded ice man and snickers for the telephone operator who had a nervous tic. Prejudice against Jews, of whom there were a few in Willow Corners, and Negroes, of whom there were none, was intense. (Schreiber 1975, 120)

A modern British case-history (Cutler and Reed 1975) again points to the importance of fundamentalist religious faith, as well as giving further evidence of the significance of an 'artistic' sensibility:

> Under the influence of her family she [Mrs AB] had, up to this time, been a devout member of the Jehovah's Witness, and had led a very restricted social life. Her four years in the services, however, saw an increase in her social activities and degree of independence from home. [. . . .] She was an avid reader, particularly of fiction and biographies. (Cutler and Reed 1975, 21)

In my opinion the reason why religion is omnipresent as an apparent causal factor in these cases is that, paradoxically, it encloses individuals in 'totalizing' beliefs in which contradiction and variation is impossible. This seems a little less paradoxical when – as I will do later – we consider the number of homogeneous, undivided characters in literature who go mad or are destroyed. It is as if the ability to lead a contradictory life enables the individual to come to terms with contradictory demands made upon him or her; any belief system which through demanding consistency renders this solution impossible will force the contradictions to manifest themselves in more final and devastating ways. As I will also argue later this perhaps explains why men – who can lead separate lives at work and at home more easily and more frequently than women – seem less subject to personality dissociation than do women. This hypothesis would also explain, incidentally, why it appears to be the case that protestant and in particular fundamentalist Christian beliefs seem frequently to be associated with personality dissociation; such belief systems seem to invade the individual's privacy more completely than, say, Catholicism.

On this point the literary evidence seems to diverge from the real-life case-histories. Of the novels and plays I consider later on only Charlotte Brontë's *Villette* highlights the issue of religious belief to any great extent. However this single case does give strong confirmatory evidence of the importance of religion to the individual faced with painful and seemingly insoluble problems. Lucy Snowe's Protestantism – as I shall argue in more detail later – comes to symbolize her right to individual privacy; to a soul secluded from the inquiring gaze of others. Her religion is of particular value to her as its stress upon the individual conscience, the private responsibility to God, allows her an inner refuge from the traumatic pressures placed upon her by other people. So far as the other literary works are concerned, I would hypothesize that the strong taboos surrounding the discussion of religious belief may be partly responsible for their lack of concern with religious belief as a possible contributory cause in cases of personality breakdown and fragmentation.

5 *Dissociation as a means of escape from otherwise insoluble problems.* Cutler and Reed (1975) give a succinct account of a patient's own understanding of the function dissociation performed for her.

> The patient's own appraisal of her illness, and particularly of her episodes of multiple personality, is that it is a 'mechanism for avoiding trouble'. She implies that the difficulty in the early stages of her illness was her insecurity, being pregnant and not married. The development of multiple personality, however, followed the birth of her first child and she now sees the difficulties of that time as revolving around her husband's isolationist attitude towards the rest of the neighbourhood and her own disappointment at being confined to a domestic life and unable to realize her own ambitions. (Cutler and Reed 1975, 23)

It is as if, here, the confinement to a home and its problems parallels the more psychic confinements of fundamentalist religion, and we note clearly the importance of gender in the account given. Evelyn Lancaster's situation, already referred to, is strikingly similar. In a seemingly impossible situation with regard to the religious upbringing of her child, the emergence of the 'Eve Black' figure who had no feelings of sympathy towards the child was clearly (for Eve Black, at any rate) an attractive solution. Eve Black was not bound by the promise because 'she' did not make it, and she felt herself to be someone different from the person who gave the undertaking. Evelyn

Lancaster, in her retrospective analysis, does not quite see it in these terms, but she recognizes that her dissociation was both a response to and a solution for irreconcilable external pressures. What is, I think, important in her analysis is that she sees the root cause of her dissociation to lie in a particular combination of internal and external factors.

> In a sense it's a way of refusing to face up to the harsh facts of life. Instead of having to find a solution to perplexing human problems – which always involve, 'Should I?' or, 'Shouldn't I?' – you just succumb and let both the pro and the con have their innings. Take good and evil. It isn't a problem that was unique with Eve White. It's a problem everyone is faced with, because everyone has good and bad impulses. Most people work out some sort of compromise between them. But others aren't able to make the compromise. Instead they avoid conflict by giving in to *both* opposing forces. They split themselves up into a good half and a bad half.
>
> When people dissociate so completely as to develop new personalities, the competing personalities are never plagued by the same conflicts and difficulties which harrass their psychic siblings. (Lancaster and Poling 1958, 119)

There is, however, something unsatisfactory in the formulation of 'good and bad impulses', because this suggests that Evelyn Lancaster could have behaved in one 'good' way, whereas the details of her experiences indicate that this was not the case. In addition to the problems concerning her child's education, she was also torn between a desire to do the best for her child and a desire to lead a fulfilling life of her own. We cannot call one of these impulses good and one bad; both were legitimate, but both could not be indulged. But the *belief* that one was good and one bad seems to have been a significant factor in dissociation, and the categorization of opposing selves as 'good' and 'bad' seems to be a not uncommon response – witness the tendency to appropriate 'Jekyll and Hyde' as a convenient label.

The division into 'Eve Black' and 'Eve White' certainly solved some problems insoluble in an undivided state. Thus Eve Black denied that the child was hers, refused to let it interfere with her pleasure, called it a 'brat' and appears on one occasion physically to have mistreated it. Compare the comments of 'Carrie', one of Mrs G's other selves:

> I think one of the things I'm going to do is to come out tonight when she [Mrs G] goes home and tell those little bastard children of hers exactly where they stand and where she stands and tell them either to put up, shut up and get out, or something. (Stoller 1974, 171)

It is revealing that 'Eve Black' was the maiden name of Evelyn Lancaster, which suggests that one of the impulses leading to dissociation was a desire to regain the independence of a pre-marital state.

Different personalities seem very often to emerge to confront problems they are suited to deal with. Talking of her family Mrs G states that having found that each one of them was different she had to be different for each of them (Stoller 1974, 97). 'Jonah', a black American male reported on by Arnold M. Ludwig and others, shifted personalities in accordance with the requirements of different situations. Thus his personality 'Sammy', the lawyer or mediator, first emerged to tell his parents not to fight in front of their children, whereas 'Usoffa Abdulla', the warrior figure, appeared when Jonah was about nine or ten and was being beaten up by a group of white boys. The authors of this study note that the experience of a strong sexual, aggressive or interpersonal conflict within Jonah serves as an 'automatic switch-over mechanism' for the evocation of the appropriate, corresponding personality (Ludwig *et al.* 1972, 308). These findings are in harmony with those drawn by Henri Ellenberger from a number of such cases:

> We should also note that with most of these patients, epileptic as well as hysterical, the appearance and disappearance of the fugue state curiously responded to the needs of certain situations. Both of Charcot's patients fell into this condition immediately after cashing appreciable sums of money; they were unable to account for the way in which they had spent it. Having returned to awareness, they felt guilty and displayed a self-punitive behavior. Charcot's second patient returned to awareness just after his 'second self' managed to escape most adroitly the consequences he might have met with for travelling beyond the station allowed by his ticket. (Ellenberger 1970, 126)

Guilt is perhaps best seen as a sort of embryo dissociation, as it necessarily involves one part of the self disapproving of another. It seems that however serious the initial pressures which contribute to the emergence of the different personalities, they can be recalled to deal with what, in comparison, appear to be relatively trivial desires and difficulties. Thus Eve Black, who liked going to dances, smoking and drinking, and – like Miss Beauchamp's Sally – lacked her alter ego's moral discretion and commitment to the standards of middle-class decorum, got into difficulties which she had to leave Eve White to cope with. Although Eve Black successfully managed to fill a job as a night-club stand-in singer for a few days, for which she had no formal qualifications or experience, she 'called in' Eve White to deal with the problem of a serviceman's aggressive sexual demands on her after she had allowed him to pick her up.

In spite of Eve Black's less repressed, more seemingly 'amoral' behaviour, she seems to have been uninterested in physical sexuality. Her impulses were all towards forms of social enjoyment of a particular stereotyped nature, to describe which an appropriately clichéd term such as 'living it up' seems needed. 'Living it up' was all that conventional views of the well-behaved young mother forbade. This form of behaviour was not unique to Evelyn Lancaster's *alter ego*; Cornelius C. Wholey (1933) notes of Mrs X, the subject of his article, that her husband related that astonishing changes in her behavior took place after her first baby came. At times he would come home to find her domestic, interested in her house, taking all a normal mother's fond care of her child. Again he would return to find the baby neglected, apparently forgotten; the mother would be out aimlessly parading the streets, gazing into shop windows, and carrying on with strange men. (Wholey 1933, 659)

Our confidence in what is, or should be, 'normal' for a young mother is probably less unchallenged now than it was in 1933, and many would perhaps wish to add something to Wholey's gloss on Mrs X's behaviour, accurate as it doubtless is in a limited way:

We can see how completely Mrs X has been able to free herself from her duties and moral standards by her unconscious assumption of the childish, carefree, irresponsible 'Susie' character. (Wholey 1933, 659)

Evelyn Lancaster, like many other individuals seeking to understand and explain their own breakdown, oscillates between attributing the blame to herself and to forces outside herself. We have already seen how, in a previous quotation, she can use the idea of 'good' and 'evil' impulses to explain her fragmentation, terms which implicitly lay the blame for her breakdown on internal causal factors. But elsewhere she is able to perceive that the lives many women lead are such as to place powerful and contradictory pressures upon them. Talking of her two main personalities – Eve White and Eve Black – she notes that Eve White, her 'moral' personality,

had a great, if unreasoning, faith in her way of life, and she had a quiet strength that made her more than a match for Eve Black for several years. If her miscarriage [*during which she reports that her husband treated her extremely badly, JH*] hadn't forced her to ask herself, 'What have I done to deserve this', I think her strength and her faith might well have carried her to the end of the path on which she'd set her feet. And, in the end, she would have gone to the grave another member of that unspectacular clan of mildly neurotic women whose anxious, taut, repressed lives earn them the final pathetic accolade, 'She was a good woman and she never complained of her lot.' (Lancaster and Poling 1958, 55)

In this last quotation Evelyn Lancaster, instead of searching inwards for 'evil' and 'good' impulses, turns her attention outwards on to wider social pressures, seeing herself not as a unique and unrepresentative oddity, but as a woman responding to pressures which affect many other 'normal' women in her society. The implications of this approach to her dissociation are important, and I would like to explore them in a separate chapter before moving to look at a number of individual literary works.

2
Personality, History and Society

Taylor and Martin conclude their survey of reported multiple personality cases with the following optimistic expression of belief concerning the usefulness of their, and others', work:

> As Francis Bacon said, 'Then only will there be good ground of hope for the further advance of knowledge, when there shall be received and gathered together into natural history a variety of experiments, which are of no use in themselves, but simply serve to discover causes and axioms; which I call *"experimenta lucifera,"* experiments of *light.'* Cases of multiple personality are natural *experimenta lucifera*. (Taylor and Martin 1944, 297)

Just as the investigation of how physical deformity in the human foetus is caused necessarily involves an understanding of the processes whereby any foetus matures and develops, so too an understanding of the factors operative in the emergence of personality dissociation cannot but throw some light upon the ways in which a 'normal' personality is formed. My inverted commas, however, suggest an immediate problem: physical normality is much easier to define than is normality of personality.

This becomes clearer when we introduce the related contexts of history and society. A modern medical investigator, examining an Egyptian mummy, feels no compunction about pronouncing upon the physical state of the long-dead individual. Of course the investigator will be aware that the norm for such things as life-expectancy, physical size, resistance to disease, and so on will vary from age to age and from society to society. Nevertheless, he or she will be unembarrassed by the need to comment in an evaluative manner on the individual's physical condition in life as indicated by his or her remains.

But given evidence of a particular person's personality traits as revealed, say, in an ancient written record, we understand I think that value judgements upon them involve a rather different and far more contextual approach. Whereas a medical investigator can make relatively simple generalizations about the need for adequate diet, exercise, protection from the weather and from infection, such trans-historical and trans-social generalizations are far more difficult to make so far as ideal social and cultural factors are concerned. I have elsewhere discussed the work of various writers who have sought to establish that there are differences in the form of characterization found in, respectively, the epic, the saga and the novel. In line with their own suggested conclusions I have argued that the far greater internal complexity of the individual character presented in the novel is related to the fact that the society from which the novel emerges consists of human beings who compete not only with nature but also with one another through their membership of opposed social classes. Of particular interest, I think, is the classic comparison Erich Auerbach makes in his *Mimesis* between the 'multilayeredness' of the individual character portrayed in the Jewish tradition (he cites as example the Biblical account of Abraham's journey to sacrifice his son), and the rather different portrayal of character by Homer (Auerbach 1971, 3–23). In Homer, Auerbach suggests, the complexity of the psychological life 'is shown only in the succession and alternation of emotions.' Given this sharp contrast, explanations are not long in seeking. The Jewish people have lived as a persecuted minority within other societies to which they do, and do not, belong. The Homeric epic, in contrast, emerged from a society less fissured, less divided against itself. As I hope to demonstrate in my later discussion of Charlotte Brontë's novel *Villette*, there is a causal link from powerlessness and oppression through to the creation of a division in the individual between the public and the private, to division within the realm of the private itself.

Social conflict is, I would argue, one of the ways in which divisions in the individual between the public and the private are encouraged. Indeed, we can say that conflict between the members of a society will tend to encourage the development of an increasingly important realm of the private. As consideration of the Homeric epic reminds us, we should not assume that all human beings have, historically, led 'private lives' in the way that members of contemporary Western capitalist societies do. Consider, for example, the very rich implications of the Biblical account of Christ's response to those who ask whether it is lawful to give tribute to Caesar:

> But Jesus perceived their wickedness, and said, Why tempt ye me, *ye* hypocrites?
> Shew me the tribute money. And they brought unto him a penny.
> And he saith unto them, Whose *is* this image and superscription?
> They say unto him, Caesar's. Then saith he unto them, Render therefore unto Caesar the things which are Caesar's; and unto God the things that are God's.
> When they had heard *these words*, they marvelled, and left him, and went their way. (Matthew 22, 18–22)

The division between the things of the state and the things of God advanced in this passage is inextricably wedded to a particular context here – a context in which the Jews had to exist within a civil power hostile to them and their religion. And as I have suggested elsewhere, the receptivity of modern Western societies to aspects of the Jewish tradition contained within the Christian religion seems in part to be associated with the existence of significant internal divisions in such contemporary societies. It is interesting that the OED gives the date of 1601 for the first usage of 'Caesar' to indicate the civil power, and refers to the account in Matthew quoted above. Reading a book such as Leo Rosten's *The Joys of Yiddish* one is struck by how much of Jewish humour relies on responses by clever individuals to the competing demands of different authorities – much, if I may say so without offence, as does the appeal of Christ's artful response to those seeking to trap him.

Historically there are, I think, three factors which above all others involve the development of increasingly complex human personalities, personalities not only divided between public and private worlds, but divided, too, within the realm of the private. The first of these I have already indicated: social conflict. Where you are in conflict with someone else then you have something to hide. The second is the development of literacy and formal education, a development which allows individuals to objectify aspects of themselves, to scrutinize themselves 'from the outside'. As A.R. Luria illustrates in his book *Cognitive Development*, the ability to engage in self-analysis is something that is developed largely through the acquisition of literacy and through formal education. Luria argues that there is every reason to think that self-awareness is a product of socio-historical development (Luria 1976, 145), and he associates the development of this ability with the acquisition of what he calls the 'higher mental activities.' Taking three groups of people studied during his research in Soviet Uzbekistan and Kirghizia in the late 1920s and 1930s – illiterate peasants from remote villages, collective farm workers who have completed short-term educational programmes, and young people who are 'farm activists' and have completed short-term educational programmes – Luria indicates a remarkable growth from the first group to the third in a willingness and ability to engage in self-analysis.

The development of literacy gives a society or an individual the means for self-analysis. It is not too much of an exaggeration to suggest that the people without literacy is a people with an identity but without a history; written records give a culture a sense of existence *and change* over time that oral records cannot achieve. For the individual the acquisition of literacy not only permits more complex and accurate forms of self-objectification and self-analysis, but it also develops higher levels of conceptual thought which again allow for a much more advanced form of self-scrutiny. Consider just one example: the ability to keep a diary. Henri Ellenberger refers to Jules Romains's argument that anyone keeping a personal diary tends to develop a dual personality that gradually emerges in that diary, so that the diarist is able to develop a 'peculiar interpersonal relationship' between him or herself and the fictitious second self (Ellenberger 1970, 169).

What it is important to add to this account is that literacy and the development of higher mental powers may produce more complex and multilayered personalities, but that only in certain circumstances will this complexity involve tension, will there be conflict between these different layers.

And this takes me to my third factor: the division of labour and the development of private property. It is clearly difficult to make an absolute distinction between this element and that of conflict, as the two are frequently very closely related. The Soviet psychologist A.N. Leont'ev refers to changes in the individual consciousness associated with the division of labour in society and with, too, 'the separation of the majority of producers from the means of production, and an isolation of theoretical activity from practical activity'. He concludes that the development of private property engenders economic alienation which, in its turn, leads to the alienation and the disintegration of human consciousness (Leont'ev 1978, 19). This is stated rather baldly here, but in the chapters following I hope to substantiate this general claim. For the moment I would ask the reader to consider the historical changes attendant upon the emergence of literacy, the sharpening of class conflict, and the accelerating division of labour in society.

It may be argued, of course, that magic, religion, and the acutely hierarchical nature of pre-capitalist societies performed much the same sort of role as that performed in industrialized societies by more recent forms of alienation. My response to this argument would be to emphasize the *public* and *fixed* nature of the divisions engendered by such older pressures. A person born a peasant in a feudal society seems not to have been subject to any pressure to be two different sorts of person; admittedly the one sort of person he or she was required to be was often far from pleasant, but as Luria's interviews with illiterate peasants show, even in the present century this does not by itself ensure that the person concerned will be impelled to become a different sort of person. In like manner the collective (if hierarchical) nature of religion and magic do not seem to have been of the nature to induce the sort of dissociation rendered more commonplace in industrial, capitalist society.

I mention A.R. Luria above, and I should perhaps stress that my arguments in this chapter are heavily dependent on insights gained from his work, and that of his teacher and colleague L.S. Vygotsky. I assume that human consciousness and personality are formed not by purely innate forces, but are moulded to a greater or a lesser extent by social and historical factors. Both Luria and Vygotsky have argued against the view that individual maturation is predominantly a matter of the individual's projecting genetically determined 'forces' into a separate and resistant society. Rather, they have argued, it is a case of our understanding socialization and maturation as processes through which the individual actively internalizes material given to him or her by society — especially through the acquistion of language. According to Vygotsky his hypothesis

establishes the unity but not the identity of learning processes and internal developmental processes. It presupposes that the one is converted into the other. Therefore, it becomes an important concern of psychological research to show how external knowledge and abilities in children become internalized. (Vygotsky 1978, 90)

Just as Vygotsky posits a complex dialectical relationship between language and thought, whereby developments in each of these in the growing child are both made possible by and also facilitate developments in the other, so too he sees maturation not as a mechanical transference of social norms on to the individual's passively receptive consciousness, but as a dynamically interactive process in which relatively internal, genetically determined elements interact and integrate with other social and cultural factors. These last are, of course, mediated through various social institutions: the family, the school, the workplace. The sophistication of the process posited is suggested in the following quotation, in which Vygotsky talks of the tension aroused in the child by desires that cannot immediately be gratified.

> To resolve this tension, the preschool child enters an imaginary, illusory world in which the unrealizable desires can be realized, and this world is what we call play. Imagination is a new psychological process for the child; it is not present in the consciousness of the very young child, is totally absent in animals, and represents a specifically human form of conscious activity. Like all functions of consciousness, it originally arises from action. The old adage that child's play is imagination in action must be reversed: we can say that imagination in adolescents and school children is play without action. (Vygotsky 1978, 93)

What is, I think, important about this hypothesis is that it allows for a complex, two-way process of influence and incorporation between the individual and society, with the individual seen neither as blank sheet of paper nor as embryonic source of a total personality. This contrasts, I think, with the behaviourist model suggested by Robert J. Kohlenberg, in which multiple personality is seen not as a splitting or fracturing of the ego, but as 'a function of the consequence of the multiple personality type behavior' (Kohlenberg 1973, 139). It will be clear that I do not see this as absolutely wrong, but I think that it represents a very complex process of to-ing and fro-ing between individual and society rather too crudely as purely one-way: from behaviour, to consciousness. The models referred to by Cutler and Reed are more sophisticated, but suffer from the opposite fault of seeing the fragmentation in too internal a manner (a fault from which their own article does not suffer, I should perhaps stress):

> The importance of role playing had previously been emphasized by Taylor and Martin (1944), the patient entering a fugue state and adopting a role from his past experience of phantasy. Congdon *et al.* (1961) report a case which clearly exhibits the gradual transition from imagined play-mate, through conscious role playing, to unconscious alternation between two roles or personalities. (Cutler and Reed 1975, 19)

I hope that by now a coherent model of the construction of personality is emerging for the reader, a model which will allow for the 'importation' of social contradictions into the individual as well as for their subsequent projection back into society. Such a model, I should stress, does not reject the view that there might be an important or even necessary role for organic dysfunction to play in the emergence of multiple personality. Dissociation might turn out to be impossible without some contributory organic factor. But this need not affect the incorporation of social elements into the resultant dissociated behaviour.

Let me make one other, general point. Ernest Hilgard accepts that the phenomenon of multiple personality represents in some sense an effort at coping with a very difficult childhood, but he goes on to suggest that 'The evidence does not favor cultural causes in the larger sense, but rather a disintegration of values at the heart of the family [. . .] (Hilgard 1977, 39). But 'the family' is not a socially or historically stable institution, nor is it clear how successfully we can separate the family from larger social factors. 'The family' and 'society' are in part involved in and constituted by each other; the values that exist (or, it is believed, should exist) within the family are organically related to aspects of the society in which the given family exists. Differences in socially accepted views of gender-roles, variations between the extended and the nuclear family, different divisions of responsibility between the family and other social institutions – all of these factors should warn us that it is difficult to see the family in glorious isolation. I do not want to deny certain obvious points: Hilgard is clearly correct (on the evidence of the many published case-histories) to stress the crucial significance of parental maltreatment of the child. But the evidence, as I hope to show, is that the contradictory forces involved in the emergence of multiple personality can have a range of different origins, and I think that Gardner Murphy's wider view, that most cases of multiple personality appear essentially to represent the organism's efforts to live, at different times, in terms of different systems of values (Murphy 1966, 451), is a more helpful one.

The wider source of the contradictions involved is, I think, seen clearly if one examines the particular case-histories. Take, for example, the case of Sybil (Schreiber 1975). Two of her personalities were 'male', which is to say that while they were in control of her Sybil spoke, behaved and thought as if she were a man.* Now in one way, of course, this indicates the extent to which the secondary personalities of those with dissociative disorders are unlike the personalities of 'normal' people: the latter don't normally develop personalities which are in conflict with their biological identity – although

---

* One of the personalities of Mrs X (Wholey 1933, 661) was also male. The fullest account of a female with a dissociated male personality is in Stoller (1974). His subject, Mrs G, believed herself to have a penis even when in an undissociated state.

this is not utterly unknown. The actual content of Sybil's 'male' utterances is, however, extremely interesting; this is 'Mike', talking to her doctor:

> 'You're getting Sybil ready to go into the world on her own. You've encouraged her in her dream of being an independent woman and making a place for herself. A teacher? Maybe. But the big jobs in education are held by men. [. . .] As far as that silly dream of being a doctor is concerned, she doesn't have what it takes. All these years of studying science subjects that haven't come naturally have gotten her nowhere. Medical schools are very selective about the women they take, and they're not going to settle for her. This is still a man's world, and women don't really have a chance. [. . .]' (Schreiber 1975, 378)

Whatever the genetic, organic or familial contributions to Sybil's dissociation, a passage like this makes it clear that larger social factors cannot be excluded from the formation of secondary personalities – just as they cannot be excluded from the construction of any personality. Comparable confirmatory evidence of this is given by Ernest Hilgard in his study of divided consciousness. Hilgard is discussing what he calls the 'hidden observer', that is, a secondary form of information processing taking place in the individual of which the dominant consciousness is unaware, but which can store information that may be made available to the primary consciousness later on either 'naturally', or as a result of hypnosis. One subject reported that she felt surprised and shocked to discover that such a 'hidden observer' existed within her consciousness, although its presence was revealed only through hypnosis. She commented of the 'hidden observer' that

> 'He seems more mature than the rest of me. More logical, and amused by the me that couldn't hear because of course you can hear.' She explained that she used the masculine pronoun for the hidden observer because she thinks of males as more logical, females as more intuitive. (Hilgard 1977, 212)

It is clear here that what are culturally determined views of gender characteristics enter in to the subject's conception of her different mental operations – maybe even determine the nature of such operations in part. In Jean Rhys's *After Leaving Mr Mackenzie* Julia Martin, having just had a telephone call asking her to come to the bedside of her dying mother, is hurrying to get ready:

> All the time she was doing this, something in her brain was saying coldly and clearly: 'Hurry, monkey hurry. This is death. Death doesn't wait. Hurry, monkey, hurry. (Rhys 1971, 86)

Why is it that the cold, clear, rational, logical part of a woman's brain should be forced to be merely a 'hidden observer'? Clearly women are capable of being rational and logical. From these examples one cannot help wondering whether it is because a woman is socialized into an intuitive, emotional, non-logical identity within many societies that her capacity for rational thought and behaviour is demoted to the function of 'hidden observer'.

In *Studies on Hysteria* both Freud and Breuer give examples which add weight to my argument at this point. In his discussion of the case of Anna O, to which I have already made reference, Breuer comments:

> even when she was in a very bad condition – a clear-sighted and calm observer sat, as she put it, in a corner of her brain and looked on at all the mad business. (Freud and Breuer 1978, 101)

More interestingly, Freud reports of Fräulein Elisabeth von R that she found intellectual stimulation from her relationship with her father, but that

> he did not fail to observe that her mental constitution was on that account departing from the ideal which people like to see realized in a girl. He jokingly called her 'cheeky' and 'cock-sure', and warned her against being too positive in her judgements and against her habit of regardlessly telling people the truth, and he often said she would find it hard to get a husband. She was in fact greatly discontented with being a girl. She was full of ambitious plans. She wanted to study or to have a musical training, and she was indignant at the idea of having to sacrifice her inclinations and her freedom of judgement by marriage. (Freud and Breuer 1978, 207)

Are Elisabeth von R's problems personal (her relationship with her father and with potential husbands) or social (the expectations her society has concerning women)? Surely they are both.

The more one studies cases of multiple personality the less satisfactory it seems to make a neat division between familial pressures and larger, social pressures on the individual. This is not to say, of course, that Hilgard and others are wrong to stress the importance of parental maltreatment in the genesis of multiple personality, but rather to add that such influences seem very often to coalesce with wider, extra-familial tensions for the child. Robert Stoller's Mrs G told him that she wanted to be a boy so that she could kill people:

> Of course, women kill people too; but men do it so much more effectively. My father was a killer, you know. The army took him out and gave him a gun and he killed people. I remember one time when I was a little kid and he was recruiting officer, and he brought home movies of the atrocities that showed people being killed in masses and shoved into pits and set on fire. Jewish people. Bodies of babies that had been mutilated. I don't know why he showed them to me. (Stoller 1974, 325)

Bruno Bettelheim's book *Paul and Mary*, dealing not with dissociation but with two children suffering from severe mental and emotional problems, tells us how Paul acted out his fantasies through games in which toy soldiers shot people (this is shortly after the Second World War), and how he rang the local museum to enquire about the 'Bikini goat' – a goat reportedly injured by radiation during nuclear tests. With Mary, the other child, such concerns were mixed up with more personal family experiences:

> Her fears that she or the School would be bombed were now connected more closely with infantile experiences. She dreamt about the war. In this dream there was an old lady who threw bombs at people when she got angry, an old lady who resembled her mother at the time when she had been sad and no longer went out. (Bettelheim 1961, 312)

Later on in the book Bettelheim mentions Mary's fascination with strangulation and the electric chair, a fascination that perhaps finds its artistic (and thus, in part, its explanatory) parallel in Sylvia Plath's *The Bell Jar*, which I shall be discussing in a later chapter.

I hope that I have now established that wider, extra-familial social tensions and contradictions cannot be excluded from the raw material from which divisions in the human personality are constructed. If maturation and socialization involve, in part, an internalizing of 'external knowledge and abilities', as Vygotsky argues, then it is logical to assume that conflicts, tensions, contradictions in the world outside the individual can be 'imported' into the individual's consciousness. If there are wars, racial tensions, cruelties in the world – whether experienced directly or indirectly – then the individual will be affected by these not just as external problems, but as problems of internal mental organization. With regard to racialism this will, I think, be seen more clearly in my later chapter concerned with literature and colonialism.

Again, if Sybil's 'Mike' is correct that the world 'he' inhabits is 'a man's world', then it is impossible to imagine how this fact can be excluded from the inner world of a woman. Few women may develop overtly male personalities in the way in which Sybil does, but their internal mental organization – if it is to relate meaningfully to the real world – will have to take this fact into account one way or another. The importance attached by the women's movement to 'consciousness raising' stems from a desire to relate to this fact in a different way, and thus to start the process of altering it.

Contradictions there may be in the individual consciousness, but there is also very clearly a drive to unity, something which clearly makes for survival value in the human individual and the human group. We try to be consistent; we try to be integrated and whole – if only to ourselves. It is thus obvious that if the individual does import contradictions into his or her consciousness then there will be a tension between these contradictions and the drive for unity. Without going too far into a complex and controversial subject it is clear that one way of resolving this tension is by some form of repression. What doesn't fit isn't acknowledged. A number of writers have examined the development of personality dissociation in terms of its being an extension of the dream process as Freud described it. Thus Erickson and

Kubie (1939) suggest that the language of Brown, the hidden second personality of their subject,

> was much like the language of dreams and constitutes in fact a demonstration of the validity of what Freud has written about the use of condensation, elision, reversal of sense, duality of meaning in the language of dreams. (Erickson and Kubie 1939, 480)

I.M. Allen (1932) makes a similar point:

> The case [of Gwen Y] suggests that restlessness during sleep, somnambulism, dissociation of personality and day-dreaming are simply varying degrees of dissociation of personality in which a complex or influence repressed during consciousness returns to active consciousness, assumes control of the personality, and influences the thoughts, speech and actions observed clinically during such phases. (Allen 1932, 329)

Where my own view diverges from such Freudian or neo-Freudian views of multiple personality as 'the return of the repressed' is that rather than seeing the secondary personality or personalities as socially unacceptable aspects of the individual that have been repressed, I would stress that what is socially acceptable may itself involve contradictory elements. This, or course, takes us back to culture and history rather than back to the pre-social ego.

Thus if, for instance, the dominant image of 'woman' in a society includes radically contradictory elements, so that the woman is enjoined simultaneously to be wife and lover, mother and sex-object, and so on, then internalization of such contradictory and irreconcilable images will involve internal conflict that has nothing to do with instinctual urges or pre-social drives. This will, I hope, be argued more convincingly in the pages that follow.

3

The Mistakes of a Night: Double Standards in *She Stoops to Conquer*

> One of John's maternal cousins, his mother's sister's daughter, a young lady of about his age, became quite unsettled mentally when twenty-five years old. She became nervous, ugly, hypochondriacal and pessimistic. She had a special antipathy to her mother, and scolded considerably. (Cutten 1903, 467)

Reading George B. Cutten's account of John Kinsel, to whose case I referred earlier, I was taken somewhat aback by the passage quoted above. The word that comes as something of a surprise in it is, I think, the word 'ugly'. We are so used to considering physical, especially sexual, attractiveness as something relatively fixed, that the idea that a change of personality can alter it seems at first sight extraordinary. 'Ugly' seems to belong to a completely different category from the other words used to describe the poor lady's changed state. And yet, as I have already noted, one of the aspects of multiple personality that is frequently commented on by investigators is the way in which different personalities of the same individual can appear to be strikingly more or less attractive. Male doctors investigating cases of multiple personality (and most of the doctors are of course male even though a majority of the subjects appear to be female), frequently comment upon the way in which a change of personality seems to inject something into the individual's total physical appearance that is hard to isolate but which has a very striking effect.

The heroine of Goldsmith's *She Stoops to Conquer* does not become ugly, although she does end the play, having won her man, 'tormenting him to the back Scene'. What is thought-provoking, however, is that Marlow, the man, finds Kate sexually exciting only in one of the two guises which she adopts in the play. Moreover, the 'two' different Kates are not just different in terms of their ability sexually to excite a man; they have complex and fascinating connections with divisions in other characters in the play, and with alternative and opposing cultural and historical values. There are few literary works which can better illustrate the subtle and complicated links between history, society and gender, and their respective divisions, interconnections, and contradictions.

On first sight I can believe that *She Stoops to Conquer* may seem an odd text to focus attention on after an extended discussion of clinically disturbed individuals. One of the staple ingredients of the village repertory theatre for several generations, few plays would seem on the surface to be more un-neurotic, more happily and unquestioningly conventional. The uncomplicated popular success of the play's first production has been repeated decade after decade, and contrasts strongly with the unintellectual, popular hostility to much modernist art and literature. And yet one does not need to be a dyed-in-the-wool Freudian to find the mistakes of a night – as the play's subtitle has it – extremely revealing concerning the tensions of the day. And as William Empson's pioneer analysis of *Alice in Wonderland* indicated, popular success does not preclude an insight into some aspects of social life and individual consciousness that are far from popular awareness.

The play was first performed in 1773 – not so long before the earliest recorded case of multiple personality – and as is not infrequently the case it uses humour to expose and investigate some relatively serious, even potentially tragic, themes. The date is important, for right from the start of the play, in the opening scene, the audience is warned that a context of social and historical change will be crucial to relationships between the different characters. Hardcastle, in this scene, tells his wife that

> I wonder why London cannot keep its own fools at home. In my time, the follies of the town crept slowly among us, but now they travel faster than a stage-coach. (Friedman 1966, 106)

This brief comment raises several important issues. Social change and, particularly, urbanization are associated with new, 'foolish' forms of behaviour. The issue of geographical mobility is significant for a number of reasons. Not only does the movement from town to country in the play involve, too, movement between two different sets of social values, but geographical mobility is a necessary element in the emergence of new forms of human privacy in the eighteenth century: people need places in which they can be private, as we shall see later. Moreover, the early dispute between Hardcastle and his wife indicates that some of the larger social tensions which I have touched upon have been to a certain extent internalized by different characters.

It is this internalization of social values of an often contradictory character that is particularly interesting about *She Stoops to Conquer*. The mistakes which lead Marlow to treat his prospective father-in-law as an innkeeper reveal one set of double standards in his attitudes to other human beings, double standards premissed upon the assumption that differences of class are equatable with more profound human differences. But related mistakes lead Marlow also to think of his prospective bride as two people, and the results of this misconception are in many ways even more interesting than the results of his misperception of Hardcastle. For it is not, the play suggests, that people behave differently in different social contexts, it is rather that their view of their own identity and of the identity of others is involved in and even partly constituted by assumptions concerning social class. The distinction is an important one, for those committed to a primarily genetic view of personality formation, who believe that the individual personality is formed as a result, largely, of innate elements, would have no difficulty in proffering a dramaturgical explanation of the fact that we behave differently in what we perceive to be different contexts. But a play which suggests that our conception of our own and other people's identities involves contradictory elements imported from society at large, and that the most apparently private and intimate feelings of sexual desire and love are mediated by, and even constituted through, complex social relationships of class and power, is saying something different from the relatively pedestrian observation that we all behave differently in different circumstances. This last banality leaves open the possibility that we remain, at bottom the same people, conscious of ourselves as integrated and whole human beings. When Marlow and Hastings treat Hardcastle as an innkeeper they are of course being made to reveal the fact that a perception of their social rank is an integral part of our perceptions of others. By contrasting their peremptory treatment of him with his own highly idealized treatment of his actual servants Goldsmith is indicating, in addition, that the 'modern' manner of behaving towards social inferiors is, unlike the 'old-fashioned' way, dehumanized and purely functional. But in the confusions of Marlow's behaviour towards Kate Hardcastle Goldsmith goes further, implying that the new element in the 'modern' is the existence not just of different, but of contradictory standards.

Significantly, this operation of double standards is associated with secrecy and hypocrisy. In Marlow's first, halting interview with Miss Hardcastle this truth is ironically revealed, the truth that Marlow's subsequent behaviour will actually enact:

> *Miss Hardcastle*: You mean that in this hypocritical age there are few that do not condemn in public what they practise in private, and think they pay every debt to virtue when they praise it.
> *Marlow*: True, madam; those who have most virtue in their mouths, have least of it in their bosoms. (Friedman 1966, 147)

It is, note, the age that is deemed to be hypocritical, an age that introduces in a sharper form this tension between private and public. To this extent both Tony Lumpkin and Hardcastle perform a similar function for Goldsmith: they are both 'of a piece', behaving and thinking the same way no matter what the context. Thus both characters function as symbols of a golden age, the last survivals of which are facing imminent extinction.

Marlow's contrasting emotions towards what he perceives as two different people – the 'servant' Kate and the 'lady' Kate – are, accordingly, set in the context of a new age in which commercial and human values, public and private norms, are in tension. Marlow's contrasting responses to the 'two' Kates clearly relate sexual attractiveness not just to physical appearance but to class identity. It is when he perceives Kate as a servant, and *because* he perceives her as such, that he is sexually excited by her. Internalized in Marlow's sexual preferences, then, are social elements; his sexuality can in no way be seen as something purely biological, but has to be recognized as saturated with social elements at every level. Part of the richness of the play lies in the fact that Kate's dual identity means different things to her father and her intended lover: to the former it represents a compromise between two ways of life and their attendant values – the old, 'organic' community of the country squirearchy and the emergent urban life of fashion and display. But to Marlow the two Kates represent different things: the Kate of her father's ideas, dressed as a housewife, is perceived as a servant, whereas the fashionable Kate is perceived as a (rather terrifying) lady. If Kate is so many different things to different people it is worth pausing to ask, at this point, what she is to herself. This is how she expresses the nature of her sartorial alternation to her father:

> *Miss Hardcastle*: You know our agreement, Sir. You allow me the morning to receive and pay visits, and to dress in my own manner; and in the evening, I put on my housewife's dress to please you. (Friedman 1966, 111)

It would seem, from this, that the Kate of the finery is the 'real' Kate, is how she actually perceives herself 'in my own manner'. But later developments in the play suggest that things are not that simple, that she herself feels divided between different manners, different sets of values, and different selves.

Marlow explains his lack of assurance with women of his own rank in a revealing exchange with Hastings, relating it to his upbringing:

> *Marlow*: [. . .] But tell me, George, where could I have learned that assurance you talk of? My life has been chiefly spent in a college, or an inn, in seclusion from that lovely part of the creation that chiefly teach men confidence. I don't know that I was ever familiarly acquainted with a single modest woman – except my mother – But among females of another class you know –
> *Hastings*: Ay, among them you are impudent enough of all conscience.
> *Marlow*: They are of *us* you know. (Friedman 1966, 129)

A number of the words used here have revealing reverberations: 'familiarly' and 'modest', for instance. Marlow's mention of his mother is also worth noting; the differential behaviour towards women that he speaks of focuses attention upon the mother, who he places in a completely different category from 'females of another class.'

Marlow's explanation for his timidity in the presence of 'modest women' – that he was brought up in seclusion from them – is not, we feel, the whole story; his final admission that 'females of another class' are 'of *us*' suggests that there is another reason for his seemingly contradictory behaviour. If it were merely a matter of one person's upbringing then Marlow would not be able to extend his point, as he does, to '*us*'.

That Marlow's contradictory response to women of differing social class is no mere personal idiosyncrasy is perhaps confirmed by the detailed criticism of the play printed in the *Morning Chronicle* on 16 March 1773 – the day after its initial performance. The newspaper critic observes that

> [. . .] Mr Marlow [is] a man of sense, education, and breeding; but, as many men are, exceedingly timid in the presence of modest women of accomplished education, impudently familiar in company with those of low degree. This character is, as far as we can recollect, an original one. The success with which it was received is a proof that it is by no means an unnatural one. (Friedman 1966, 91)

Marlow's 'split personality' is, then, one that his audience recognized. What is its basis?

To answer this question I believe that we need to go back to the two systems of social behaviour with which the play opens. Marlow is a man whose behaviour to women is premissed upon two different systems of value: one in which they are treated as human beings who merit a human response, and one in which they are treated as objects to be made use of, and whose rights are to be measured in commercial rather than in human terms. If this seems too crude an assertion it is worth looking closely at the actual language Marlow uses when talking to Hastings about Kate. Soon after his first interview with her he admits that Hastings has

> [. . .] talents and art to captivate any woman. I'm doom'd to adore the sex, and yet to converse with the only part of it I despise. (Friedman 1966, 131)

Marlow may be sexually attracted towards the 'servant' Kate, but when he describes her as 'the tempting, brisk, lively little thing that runs about the house with a bunch of keys to its girdle' he reveals the extent to which for him she is more object than person. Perhaps this suggests why he feels no shyness in her presence: an object makes no human demands upon one – a human being does. Kate may have 'Such fire, such motion, such eyes, such lips', but the same motion, eyes and lips in the 'lady' Kate induce no sexual excitement in him at all. At this point, when Hastings expresses surprise that he might be contemplating robbing a woman of her honour, he exclaims

> Pshaw! pshaw! we all know the honour of the bar-maid of an inn. I don't intend to *rob* her, take my word for it, there's nothing in this house, I shan't honestly *pay* for. (Friedman 1966, 178)

It is true that at a crucial point later on in the play Marlow recognizes Kate's humanity before he has penetrated her disguise, but this does not obscure the fact that although she may be an exception, for most women he operates according to two contradictory standards.

As I suggested earlier, Kate herself is by no means free of comparable contradictions. She dreads her first meeting with Marlow as she fears that it will be

> [. . .] so like a thing of business, that I shall find no room for friendship or esteem. (Friedman 1966, 111)

The use of business terminology here to describe a particular sort of social intercourse is revealing, and suggests that there is a felt need to distinguish the truly human from the merely commercial. Kate's 'friendship' clearly excludes 'business' here, and yet later on in the play, when she is planning to be seen by Marlow so as to interest him in her, she lets drop the opinion that being seen is

> no small advantage to a girl who brings her face to market. (Friedman 1966, 169)

It is worthy of note that in his previous play, *The Good Natur'd Man*, Goldsmith had had Honeywood use a reference to carrying one's face to market to pour scorn on a commercial approach to marriage, a scorn all of a piece with the same character's rejection of the importation of bourgeois competition into matters of the heart ('I'm no man's rival'). Miss Richland may tell Honeywood that

> Our sex are like poor tradesmen, that put all their best goods to be seen at the windows (Friedman 1966, 64)

but it is clear that implicit in the tone of this statement is a regret that the ethics of shopkeeping should corrupt sexual love.

Why is it that only a series of 'mistakes' can bring the contradictions of which I have spoken to light in this play? In part it must be because the contradictory halves of Marlow's character are normally kept safely apart. Innkeepers, for gentlemen, are not normally the fathers of potential wives, and women are never normally both servant girls and ladies, and thus the contradictions are never exposed. Strict social and (bearing in mind the function of the contrast between London and the countryside), geographical barriers keep different value systems apart. This is why mistakes are needed to unmask hypocrisy, a hypocrisy that is not so much personal as social in the world of *She Stoops to Conquer*. But the very concern of the play with these concealed tensions suggests that their presence was widely felt even if it was not widely admitted. Furthermore the play sets itself the function, through Marlow, of reconciling the contradictory elements. As Mr Hardcastle tells Kate,

> [. . .] if young Mr Brazen can find the art of reconciling contradictions, he may please us both, perhaps. (Friedman 1966, 161)

It is not, eventually, Marlow who reconciles the contradictions. It is Goldsmith, who reveals that the play has, after all, only been concerned with the mistakes of a night. The very title of the play has a powerful ideological thrust; female submission is acceptable because it is a means whereby dominance is achieved.

What has all this to do with multiple personality? To answer this, I would suggest that we remember that the sort of contradictions I have indicated may not always be so easily reconciled, or even separated. A society in which collective and competitive elements can be kept in different compartments can perhaps maintain both; but a society in which the collective and the competitive become increasingly confused and intermingled will produce individuals torn in different ways, individuals who have internalized conflicts that have become, in a fundamental sense, their own. It is my contention that this sort of confusion and interpenetration becomes more and more of a problem in Britain (and, in different ways, in other capitalist countries) as the nineteenth century progresses, until by the beginning of the twentieth it has become so sharp that the honest and perceptive artist cannot but be affected by it in his or her portrayal of character. Such an argument rests, admittedly, on evidence achieved by literary critical means from representative texts, but it also appeals to an analysis of socio-economic development which sees, in what could be called a classical Marxist view, increasing conflict between the forces and the relations of production. Put another way, the fact that human beings collaborate in production and compete in ownership of the means of production involves an increasing tension as the private ownership of the means of production holds back, rather than develops, the forces of production. As this occurs we see an increasing awareness of a tension *within* people between the cooperative and the competitive mode.

That this is not just a piece of Marxist dogma can perhaps be suggested by reference to a work written over two hundred years later than *She Stoops to Conquer*. *Love and Commitment* by Gary Schwarz and Don Merten (1980) is, in their words, 'a book about the meanings of love and intimacy in mainstream American culture'. In it the authors follow the subject of the book, 'Cheryl' (the pseudonym of a real American individual), through the 'dating' of adolescence up to her marriage. Their approach is not a Marxist one, yet they recognize, early on in the study, that there is a dialectic between an individual's feelings, thoughts and personality, and the social world to which that individual belongs.

> there is invariably an implied social referent to any 'subjective' state of mind, and, correlatively, every social situation can be characterized by the mode of consciousness it arouses in those who experience it. What we think and feel and what we believe and do are not exclusive properties of either the self or the society. Rather, thoughts and feelings, beliefs and actions arise out of and are constituted by the intersubjective understandings that are embedded in the language of ordinary discourse and that characterize the experience of everyday life. (Schwarz and Merten 1980, 15)

Given that the values of the society at large are not separate from those that constitute and distinguish the individual, it is clearly important to appreciate what the dominant values of society are. According to Schwarz and Merten,

> In American culture, there is a pervasive tension between the values of self-interest and individualism, on the one hand, and of mutuality and cooperation on the other hand. The tension between them is neither easily balanced nor readily resolved. Our culture gives higher priority to self-interest and individualism that it does to mutuality and cooperation. (Schwarz and Merten 1980, 26)

In response to such tensions, according to Schwarz and Merten, Americans tend to operate in society according to one of three basic models at any given time: the exchange, the solidarity, and the pragmatic perspectives. As the last-named of these does not seem to be all that successfully defined, and in practice consists of strategies to enable tacking between the demands of individualism and of cooperation (which thus puts it, really, into a different category from the perspectives of exchange and solidarity), I shall ignore it.

According to the two writers, few people recognize that there is an incompatibility between these two perspectives of exchange and solidarity, a lack of recognition which is understandable as, in their words, 'Our culture supports the illusion that a person can combine symbols of solidarity and exchange.' So far as Cheryl's relationships with men are concerned, this illusion leads to problems:

> Cheryl is not aware of the fact that when youth in Westwood look at dating as a public activity, the norms associated with the exchange perspective usually dominate their orientation toward intimate relationships. The sexual side of dating is perceived as a game in which each partner tries to maximize gains and contain losses. However, any boy or girl, looking at his or her dating relationship as a private matter, tends to view intimacy in terms of a solidarity perspective. (Schwarz and Merten 1980, 119)

There are elements here that are familiar from our discussion of *She Stoops to Conquer*, but there are also significant differences. The opposition between the public and the private, and the conflicting claims of what I called 'human' and 'commercial' values are reminiscent of *She Stoops to Conquer*. But whereas, in that play, the tension between these conflicting value systems comes into the open only as a result of the fortuitous bringing together of areas of experience normally kept safely apart by Marlow, in Cheryl's case the insulation of the two sets of values is a more complex matter. 'Solidarity' and 'exchange' values have been more thoroughly internalized by the members of Cheryl's society, and their separation is effected not by rigid geographical or class barriers, but by more sophisticated, shifting divisions the individual has to construct internally to wall off the public from the private. Very often this walling-off process is only partly successful; as Schwarz and Merton put it, rather tentatively,

> [. . .] many people experience what we have called the encroachment of the public on private culture. Their flow of solidarity experience is disrupted by thinking about what one is getting out of or putting into an intimate relationship. (Schwarz and Merten 1980, 254)

Indeed, as they add later on in their book, whereas the ideology of contemporary American society has it that in general 'private experiences of solidarity' penetrate the public domain (how often do we come across the myth that love can conquer all – which it clearly cannot!) in practice it is more usual for the reverse to occur. As they admit, 'solidarity in this culture is vulnerable to transformation by exchange principles, but exchange principles are extremely resistant to appeals to solidarity considerations' (Schwarz and Merten 1980, 255).

Goldsmith's treatment of the theme of benevolence, especially in *The Vicar of Wakefield* and *The Good Natur'd Man* shows that he was aware of a not dissimilar situation in his own society; benevolence has to be kept secret, protected by rich uncles, or it will be exploited by those living by the principles of exchange and will destroy its possessor. This same insight is to be found in Brecht's *The Good Person of Setzuan* where the heroine has, again, to become two people in order to protect herself from the exploitation of her good qualities by others.

If there are similarities between Goldsmith's society and Brecht's, however, there are also important differences. In the century and a half separating the two writers the conflict between communality and individualism, between cooperation and competition, has sharpened. Not only does this mean that there are powerful social forces publicly identified with world-views sympathetic to either cooperation or competition, but it also means that the conflict between these two has been further internalized by human beings. This, as we will see, leads to additional technical problems for the writer who wishes to portray human beings in their entirety.

4

Double Lives: Dostoyevsky, Hawthorne, Stevenson, Dickens and Gaskell

This is not a book concerned specifically with the topic of the double in literature. It is clear, however, that an increased interest in the portrayal of doubles on the part of a significant number of writers in a given period bespeaks some sort of concern with the issue of individual identity, and this in turn suggests that something is making this issue more problematic for these writers than it was, perhaps, for writers of a different period. Introducing his translation of Otto Rank's classic work *The Double* (Rank 1979), Harry Tucker Jr comments upon the striking tripartite conjunction of interest in the theme of the literary double, major upheavals of society, and the development of psychology in its recognizably modern form. We might add to this list the medical profession's discovery of – and increasing concern with – multiple personality.

Tucker points out that there have been periods of social upheaval (he refers to the Thirty Year's War) during which the theme of the double either did not appear in literature or was insignificant (Rank 1979, xx), and so we should avoid positing any mechanical relationship between social upheaval and literary convention or subject matter. Clearly fashion may play some element in the popularity of the double theme in certain historical periods – as Arnold M. Ludwig and others suggest is also true of the diagnosis of multiple personality (Ludwig *et al.* 1972, 298). But 'fashion' is itself a problematic concept; what is fashionable may be partly a matter of accident, but it is hard to believe that no isolable causal factors enter into the determination of the fashion that dominates an art form at a particular time.

Ralph Tymms, in his important *Doubles in Literary Psychology* (1949), sees the roots of the theme of the double in the ordinary phenomenon of family likeness and chance resemblance, but he adds that these roots 'will also be seen to be firmly embedded in magic and in the earliest speculations on the nature of the soul' (Tymms 1949, 15). He further suggests that there is a complex relationship between the development of modern psychology, the 'Mesmerist's observation of hitherto unsuspected traits of character', and the great development of interest in doubles in the literature of the Romantic period. Like Tucker, then, he perceives a family of traits, including the development of psychology, literary romanticism and social change, to be involved in the eruption of interest in the portrayal of literary doubles. It would seem that the development of psychology can be seen both as effect and as cause; a feeling that human consciousness was complex and concealed enough to merit analysis perhaps contributes to the development of the discipline, but the findings of psychological inquiry react back on to people's conception of the nature of human consciousness and individual identity.

Tymms quotes some interesting links between psychological writings of the Romantic period and literary figures, which indicate that in some cases a direct influence seems to be traceable from psychological inquiry to literary creation:

> In *Die Symbolik des Traumes*, G.H. Schubert (whose lectures Kleist attended in Dresden) quotes from the standard works on magnetism available to him – not all of which would be accessible to Kleist, but which correspond to the theories of magnetic phenomena in vogue at the period. Schubert mentions women whose lives were divided into separate, alternating parts, with completely different characteristics [. . .]. (Tymms 1949, 46)

Claims involving such direct 'influences' have to be treated with some circumspection; whatever they offer, it is not any sort of final answer to the significance of the double in Romantic – or other – literature. We have to ask what led the Mesmerists to conduct their experiments in the first place, and why writers were willing to be influenced by the published results of such experiments.

Both C.F. Keppler in his book *The Literature of the Second Self* (1972), and Robert Rogers in his book *The Double in Literature* (1970), have considered the varying ways in which different writers have utilized the double or second self in their work. Many of their individual analyses are extremely illuminating, but in both works I feel the need for more stress on the historical determinants at work in the literary portrayal of the double. To this end I would like now to turn to the portrayals of doubles, split-identities, and 'secret lives' in the works of five major nineteenth-century novelists. Dostoyevsky's *The Double* is a very obvious starting-point, as in it the Russian author focuses attention on the theme that is to dominate all of his writing: the divided nature of human consciousness, split between the 'public' and the 'underground'. A number of critics have referred to a passage in *A Raw Youth* in which Dostoyevsky specifically refers to clinical cases of dissociation:

> What then precisely is the 'double'? The 'double', at any rate according to a medical work by an expert which I afterwards read for the purpose, is nothing but the first stage in some serious mental derangement which may lead to a pretty bad conclusion. (quoted in Coleman 1934, 267)

Dostoyevsky, then, at some stage in his writing career clearly knew something of the existence of clinical dissociation. But it is important to stress that his whole life's work is concerned with the question of opposing elements in human individuals, and that he *uses* information from clinical case-histories to illuminate what is presented in his works as a far more widespread duplicity in the characters he portrays. Even when he presents his readers with a character who is undivided, honest and 'good', like the Prince in his *The Idiot*, the underlying literary aim is to explore the impossibility of such a person in his contemporary world.

We need, then, to see *The Double* as a novel which uses information perhaps partly gained from clinical case-histories to explore more socially representative forms of duplicity and contradiction, rather than as a novel which sets out to investigate a particular neurotic or disturbed condition. Dostoyevsky appears to use the knowledge of such clinical cases of dissociation as were available to him to make Golyadkin's character psychologically convincing, however. According to Joseph Frank,

> the novel originally contained a passage that explicitly motivates Golyadkin as engaging in ego-enhancing daydreams. Mr Golyadkin, Dostoevsky wrote, 'very much loved occasionally to make certain romantic assumptions touching his person; he liked to promote himself now and then into the hero of the most ingenious novel, to imagine himself entangled in various intrigues and difficulties, and, at last, to emerge with honor from all the unpleasantnesses, triumphing over all obstacles, vanquishing difficulties and magnanimously forgiving his enemies' (Frank 1977, 301)

Golyadkin is, then, just the sort of nervous, introverted character who we have seen to be vulnerable to personality dissociation. He also, incidentally, resembles Conrad's Lord Jim, who as a youth indulges in fantasies of heroic deeds, and as an adult speaks of his fatal jump as of the action of another person – almost a double.

It also emerges, in the later text of the novel (which is the one available in English translation), that Golyadkin has been under considerable strain for some time at work and in his relationships, real or imagined, with one or more women. The actual appearance of the double is also preceded by a profound crisis in his life which, again, is as we have seen typical of the non-literary cases of multiple personality we have looked at:

> Mr Golyadkin, seeing that Andrey Philippovich had recognized him beyond doubt and was staring with all his might, so that he could not hope to remain concealed, blushed to the roots of his hair. 'Ought I to bow? Should I speak to him or not? Ought I to acknowledge our acquaintance?' our hero wondered in indescribable anguish. 'Or shall I pretend it's not me but somebody else strikingly like me, and look as if nothing's the matter?' said Mr Golyadkin, lifting his hat to Andrey Philippovich and not taking his eyes off him. 'I. . . . It's all right', he whispered, hardly able to speak, 'It's quite all right; this is not me at all, Andrey Philippovich, it's not me at all, not me, and that's all about it.' (Dostoyevsky 1972, 132)

According to Ralph Tymms, Dostoyevsky's principle source of psychological data was 'an old-fashioned work on romantic lines, *Psyche, zur Entwicklungsgeschichte der Seele*, by Carl Gustav Carus', which was published in 1846, and which was based on the theories of animal magnetism popularized by G.H. Schubert (Tymms 1949, 98). But as he began work on *The Double* in 1845 (according to Jessie Coulson, translator of the work), such an influence can only have been operative after the germ of the story had begun to mature in his mind.

Moreover, as Dmitri Chizhevsky points out in his 'The Theme of the Double in Dostoyevsky' (in Wellek 1962), in 1859 Dostoyevsky, talking about the theme of the double, remarked: 'Why should I abandon an excellent idea, a type of great social importance, which I was the first to discover and of which I was the first prophet?' To seek for wider social meaning in the theme of the double in Dostoyevsky's work is, then, not to impose on it critical theories or assumptions which Dostoyevsky would have seen to be irrelevant. If accounts of multiple personality influenced Dostoyevsky, then they did so after he had become interested in the theme of the double, and they were part of a family of ideas concerning the complexity of human personality which for Dostoyevsky, at least later on in his life, had a social significance. Joseph Frank points out that in *Poor Folk*, written prior to *The Double*, at the point where Devushkin in complete despair is summoned for his interview with the General, his feelings are described as follows:

> 'My heart began shuddering within me, and I don't know myself why I was so frightened; I only know that I was panic-stricken as I had never been before in all my life. I sat rooted to my chair – as though there were nothing the matter, as though it were not I' [. . .] Here is exactly the reaction of terror that leads to the splitting of Golyadkin's personality and the appearance of the double [. . .]. (Frank 1977, 298)

This passage was certainly written before Dostoyevsky had read Carus's book.

In both cases the experience of terror that ushers in a sense of personality loss or estrangement is given a clear social setting: it is in the presence of a superior who has a particular social authority with regard to the 'split' individual. This links up with Golyadkin's subsequent fear, immediately after meeting the double for the first time, that

> It would be terrible going into the office again. He had a strong foreboding that it was precisely there that something was wrong. (Dostoyevsky 1972, 174)

Golyadkin is an individual who is torn between conflicting demands: the demands of subservience to an arrogant, mechanical and unfeeling authority, and the demands of the truly human. As Dmitri Chizhevsky points out

The appearance of the double and his success in squeezing out Golyadkin from his place only shows that Golyadkin's place was completely illusory to begin with. For even the double can keep all his 'places' – from the office to his Excellency's cabinet – only through the purely external traits of his character: by the flattery and servility which the older Golyadkin would have liked to master himself but which are no less superficial, unessential, and inhuman and incapable of ensuring him a 'place' in life. (Wellek 1962, 116)

It is the impossibility of uniting these contradictory demands in a single, consistent, integrated personality that we see personified in an exaggerated form in the two Golyadkins.

In her undergraduate study of the theme of the double in *The Double* and *The Brothers ·Karamazov* Sylvia Plath points out that Golyadkin's immediate response to the double is paradoxical. In spite of his anxiety, she notes, he himself admits that it is as if a hundred tons had been lifted from his chest. She suggests that the reason for this relief is that his hitherto repressed and starved desires may now be satisfied. But this relief is temporary and partial:

By creating a Double, the schizophrenic no longer needs to castigate himself or to feel guilty for harboring these corrupt urges; at least he can blame someone else for transgressions which he once felt were his.

However, the advantages of this radical division involve danger as well as distinct relief. The double alleviation of tension, which frees the victim from responsibility for his repressed desires and yet satisfies those desires, is countered by a new fear of attack from the outside. (Plath 1955, 17)

Plath's view of Golyadkin's double as the 'return of the repressed', in Freudian terminology, is echoed by Robert Rogers who argues that

It is clear that Golyadkin Sr, who entertains a romantic, idealistic attitude toward women, represses his instinctual impulses; he sees his double as a lecher. (Rogers 1970, 35)

There is certainly some textual authority for such views. After reading Vakhrameyev's letter accusing him of having mistreated Karolina Ivanovna, Golyadkin, we are told,

remained for a considerable time sitting motionless on the sofa. A new light was breaking through the cloud of obscurity and mystery that had enveloped him for the past two days. It was partly that our hero was beginning to remember. . . . (Dostoyevsky 1972, 225, ellipsis in original)

The mental process here depicted does strongly suggest the return to consciousness of sexually motivated behaviour the memory of which has been repressed by Golyadkin, and the eccentric behaviour associated with Clara

Olsufyevna is also strongly suggestive of a sexual fantasy which has over-come its originator. The medical advice given to Golyadkin at the start of the story, that he should not 'stay at home all the time' (Dostoyevsky 1972, 135) also suggests that, like the hero of *White Nights*, he has replaced a real life in the outside world with a fantasy life that has, eventually, destroyed his hold upon normality. But although these elements of repressed sexuality clearly enter into Golyadkin's dissociation, there is more to the latter than the return of unacknowledged lust.

Erik Krag, in his *Dostoyevsky The Literary Artist* (1976) has indicated how much Dostoyevsky owed to Gogol in *The Double*, and notes that the parallels between *The Double* and, in particular, Gogol's *The Nose* and *The Overcoat* were such that a contemporary Russian reader would have easily recognized them (and was meant to do so). In the translated version of *The Double*, based on Dostoyevsky's revised text, many references to noses have been deleted, as if Dostoyevsky wished to play down the debt he owed to Gogol. It seems apparent, however, that ideas from *The Nose* set Dostoyevsky's imagination working: the idea that part of a man could leave him and lead an independent life, interfering with his social and, particularly, sexual relationships, must have struck important chords in Dostoyevsky's mind. The nose, of course, has always had important sexual connotations; not only is it often (as in *Tristram Shandy*) used as an analogue for the penis, but 'losing one's nose' is the result of syphilis, and thus serves as a public and visible sign that private and perhaps illicit sexual behaviour has been indulged in.

In his interesting book on literature and metamorphosis, *The Gaping Pig*, Irving Massey makes a couple of points concerning *The Nose* which it is perhaps worth pondering with regard to *The Double*. Firstly he suggests that the nose is a byword for status in a host of expressions, and that its separation from its owner in Gogol's story represents the gaining of a desired status which then leaves the self behind in an uncomfortable superfluity, without any role. Secondly, that the detachment of Kovalyov's nose 'is a kind of pro-tective imitation', in which 'one takes on the deadness of the meaningless thing or situation with which one is confronted and meets its threat by becoming it' (Massey 1976, 64). As I have suggested, these comments are peculiarly apt with regard to Golyadkin, for once he gains the status he clearly desires so much, in the shape of his double, his remaining self is rendered superfluous and with no role in life at all. And there is also a case for seeing the madness which his dissociation represents as a form of protective reaction to a life with which he can no longer cope; the end of the tale is the end of all his hopes, true, but it is also the end of all his problems.

But in some ways Gogol's *The Overcoat* seems to represent an even more significant source for certain elements in *The Double* than does *The Nose*. Aikeky Aikeyevitch is, like Golyadkin, persecuted at the office, and has to assert his essential humanity to stop the young clerks from cruelly teasing him. There is an important parallel scene in *The Double* in which

Golyadkin's encounter with two junior colleagues away from the office startles Golyadkin into acting a part foreign to his actual feelings:

> 'Yakov Petrovich, Yakov Petrovich,' twittered the two young clerks, 'you here? What has . . .?'
> 'Ah, it's you, gentlemen!' Mr Golyadkin hurriedly interrupted them, somewhat disconcerted and scandalized by the clerks' amazement and at the same time by the familiarity of their address, but involuntarily acting the free-and-easy good fellow all the same. (Dostoyevsky 1972, 146)

Golyadkin's disconcertment, it becomes clear, arises from his revealing aspects of himself to his colleagues that he normally conceals at work. Dostoyevsky, then, uses this encounter with the two clerks in a rather different way from the scene Gogol gives us of Aikeky Aikeyevitch being teased by his fellow-workers. Here the encounter, like a later encounter in Dickens's *Great Expectations* between Wemmick and Jaggers, which I will look at later, revolves around the unintended display of 'human' characteristics to 'work' colleagues; the latter ask Golyadkin how he comes to be 'scented and pomaded like this, and all dressed up', and Golyadkin, significantly, has to admit to 'another side'.

> 'You all know me, gentlemen, but up till now you have only known one side of me. Nobody is to blame for that, and I admit it is partly my own fault.' (Dostoyevsky 1972, 147)

Golyadkin's earlier claims to openness and a lack of duplicity, then, have to be taken with a pinch of salt.

The scene in *The Double* which most directly parallels Gogol's description of the teasing of Aikeky Aikeyevitch involves not an encounter between Golyadkin and his colleagues, however, but one between Golyadkin and himself – his double.

> The man now sitting opposite Mr Golyadkin was Mr Golyadkin's horror, he was Mr Golyadkin's shame, he was Mr Golyadkin's nightmare of the previous day; in short, he was Mr Golyadkin himself – not the Mr Golyadkin who now sat in his chair with his mouth gaping and the pen frozen in his grasp; not the one who liked to keep in the background and bury himself in the crowd; not, finally, the one whose demeanour said so clearly, 'Leave me alone and I'll leave you alone,' or, 'Leave me alone; I'm not interfering with you, am I?' (Dostoyevsky 1972, 177)

The phrases in inverted commas are almost identical to those uttered by the hero of *The Overcoat* to his tormentors, and it seems apparent that Dostoyevsky wanted his readers to recognize this – and that it was now a dissociated part of himself that torments the hero. The conflict has been internalized, has gone underground. There is a further odd parallel to be found in Jean Rhys's *After Leaving Mr Mackenzie*, where the appalling Uncle Griffiths reads in Julia Martin's eyes the message: 'Oh, for God's sake, leave me alone. I'm not troubling you; you've no right to trouble me. I've as much right as you to live, haven't I?' (Rhys 1971, 93). Significantly, Uncle Griffiths and Julia disagree about Dostoyevsky – he rejecting a view of the world seen through an epileptic's eyes, she suggesting that Dostoyevsky might see things very clearly.

Stanley M. Coleman, noting that *The Double* is the first of Dostoyevsky's novels to explore the subject of the mind in conflict with itself, argues that for Dostoyevsky the divided mind is never alternating personality – repression with amnesia – but is always the simultaneous presentation of conflicting feelings and impulses (Coleman 1934, 265). It is true that the only mention of possible amnesia concerns the mental stirrings that Vakhrameyev's letter causes Golyadkin. But this apart I think that in general Coleman is without any doubt correct to insist upon the fact that Golyadkin suffers from simultaneous contradictory feelings and impulses which oppress him. One sign of this is that – as a cursory glance at the novel will reveal – he talks to himself, argues with himself, continuously. On one level this is a sign of his isolation (he has hardly anyone else *to* talk to), but on another level it represents an internalization of external conflicts; he talks about problems concerning his behaviour in the external world. We talk to ourselves, normally, to solve problems; without problems our cerebration is rarely consciously verbal. But talking to oneself is not for nothing referred to in popular myth as 'the first sign of madness'. Golyadkin's inner speech serves, paradoxically, further to bifurcate his life: it divides him up into a seething inner mass of problems, and a halting, inarticulate public persona. This, of course, is not an accurate picture of the double, who represents a possible solution to all Mr Golyadkin's problems so far as his public behaviour is concerned, but which Golyadkin's honesty and humanity will not allow him consciously to adopt. This, if one likes, is the parallel to the force of repression that we saw constantly operating in our case-histories. Paradoxically, it is Golyadkin's attempted refusal to be double that makes him double; because he would rather not dissemble and operate according to double standards, he breaks apart.

> '[. . .] I am not an intriguer – and I am proud of that, too. I don't do things on the sly, but openly, without guile, and although I might do harm, like other people, [. . .]' (Dostoyevsky 1972, 137)

Golyadkin seems to be torn between a desire to shine in society in a way hitherto foreign to his nature, or his apparent nature, and a wish to present himself as simple, uncomplicated, of-a-piece. In his early interview with his doctor these opposing elements are clearly apparent:

> '[. . .] There, Christian Ivanovich, in society, I say you must learn how to polish the parquet with your shoes . . .' (here Mr Golyadkin scraped his foot lightly over the floor); it's expected of you, sir, and you're expected to make puns, too . . . you have to be able to produce a well-turned

compliment . . . that's what's expected of you. And I've not learnt to do all that, Christian Ivanovich, I've never studied all those clever tricks; I had no time. I am a simple, uncomplicated person, and it isn't in me to shine in society. [. . .]' (Dostoyevsky 1972, 136; ellipses in original)

As Golyadkin's later, assumed, finery reveals, in one sense this wish to shine in society clearly *is* 'in' him, however, and is demanding to be let out. This inner conflict is revealed in a number of different ways in this early interview with the doctor, and it is clear from these that Robert Roger's assertion that decomposition in literature, like dissociation and autoscopy in clinical practice, 'always reflect[s] psychosexual conflict, however obliquely', is not the case. As I have argued earlier, sexual repression seems to enter into Golyadkin's fragmentation, but this is not the whole story. Take the following complex piece of duplicity on Golyadkin's part: he is talking again to the doctor.

'Yes, somebody I know very well congratulated somebody else whom I also know very well, and who is, moreover, a friend, as it is termed, of the object of my affections, on being promoted, receiving the rank of Assessor. This is how he put it. "I feel really glad," he said, "of this opportunity to offer you my congratulations, my *sincerest* congratulations, Vladimir Semyonovich, on your promotion. And I am all the more delighted because nowadays, as all the world knows, a lot of maundering old women have been getting promotion." ' Here Mr Golyadkin nodded his head slyly and looked at Christian Ivanovich with a frown. (Dostoyevsky 1972, 141)

As is apparent from a later slip of Golyadkin's, the 'somebody' is in fact himself, and the comment about maundering old women is meant to be a hit against his sexual rival. But sexual jealousy is mixed up with other things here; professional competition and duplicity to a business superior.

In Golyadkin's *telling* this anecdote to his doctor, however, we can surely see a desire to re-establish his integrity, to bring the different parts of his life together. Talking, later on in the novel, to Anton Antonovich, Golyadkin puts forward 'the notion' that 'people wearing masks have ceased to be a rarity, sir, and that it is difficult nowadays to recognize the man under the mask' (Dostoyevsky 1972, 199). This statement seems to relate both to a realization that he himself masks some of his impulses and characteristics and also to a genuine desire that such double standards as necessitate the wearing of masks should be ended. Golyadkin's comments on masks are worth remembering, later on, when we consider important references to masks and masking in the work of Charlotte Brontë and Jean Rhys.

In one sense, then, and in spite of his duplicity, Golyadkin belongs to a long line of literary characters who are broken through a refusal to operate according to dual standards. Consider Stevie in Conrad's *The Secret Agent*, Septimus in Virginia Woolf's *Mrs Dalloway*, and Meursault in Camus's *The*

Outsider. All of these refuse to divide themselves, reject hypocrisy – and are destroyed as a result. Arnold M. Ludwig *et al*. (1972), writing about the new, integrated personality of their subject 'Jonah', note that unfortunately,

> some of the results indicate that this new identity may be psychiatrically 'sicker' than any of the others [. . .]. This would imply that the separate functioning of alter identities may represent a more effective way of handling anxiety than a coalescence of identities. (Ludwig *et al*. 1972, 310)

Golyadkin's case suggests that it may, indeed, be a more effective way of handling a particular sort of reality. Golyadkin's collapse is precipitated, after all, not by his having divided himself into two, but by his inability to keep these separate parts of himself distinct.* It is his meeting, early on, with Andrey Philippovich, which causes him to wish to be someone else. Although his life is already divided between his 'office self' and his 'private self' – the person he thinks of himself as in his imagination – he is also possessed of a strong impulse to achieve some sort of consistency and unity, an impulse evidenced, it would seem, by his visit to the doctor. Irving Massey makes a very similar point to this when, referring to such stories as *Dracula, Dr Jekyll and Mr Hyde*, and Mérimée's 'Lokis,' he suggests that he would like

> to shift the emphasis from the familiar areas of discussion of the double (such as split personality, or the suppressed natural man) to what one might rather call the discussion of the single. In other words, I would suggest that the problems in these situations arise from the unity rather than from the duality of character. (Massey 1976, 98)

As I have already indicated, Dostoyevsky wrote that he saw the double as a 'type of great social significance;' and the social and historical context of Golyadkin's bifurcation is immediately relevant to its full understanding. Discussing another of Dostoyevsky's stories – *White Nights* – A.N. Leont'ev argues that

> a historically arising separation of internal theoretical activity not only gives rise to a one-sided development of personality but may lead to psychological disorders, to splitting of personality into two spheres strange to each other – the sphere of its appearance in real life and the sphere of its appearance in the life that exists only as an illusion, only in autistic thought. It is impossible to describe such a psychological disturbance more penetratingly than did Dostoyevsky; from a wretched existence filled with senseless matters, his hero escapes into a life of the imagination, into dreams; before us there are as if two personalities, one, the personality of a man who is humiliatingly cowardly, an eccentric who

---

* Compare Fred Kaplan's point that the waking and dream worlds of Dickens's Mrs Gamp are the same; she has 'divided herself into two in order to be one and to deprive her of that other is to deprive her of herself' (Kaplan 1975, 127).

shuts himself off in his den, the other, a romantic and even a heroic personality open to all the joys of life. (Leont'ev 1978, 135)

From other writings of Dostoyevsky it seems clear that the phenomenon of talking to oneself was seen by him to have a social rather than a purely individual significance; it is not simply that the hero of *White Nights*, or Golyadkin, escape from society in their dreams and inner conversations, but rather that society pursues them in these activities. In *Crime and Punishment*, in which Raskolnikov leads a life cut off from social intercourse not dissimilar to that led by the hero of *White Nights*, the activity of talking to oneself is given a specifically social significance: talking to Raskolnikov, Svidrigaylov tells him:

And another thing. I'm convinced there are lots of people in Petersburg who talk to themselves while they walk. It's a city of semi-lunatics. If we had been a scientific nation, our doctors, lawyers, and philosophers could have made valuable investigations, each in his own field, in Petersburg. You won't often find a place like Petersburg where so many strange, harsh and gloomy things exert an influence on a man's mind. Think what the influence of the climate alone is worth. And in addition, it is the administrative centre of Russia, and its character must be reflected in everything. (Dostoyevsky 1974, 478)

Svidrigaylov goes on to describe Raskolnikov's behaviour when he leaves the house and walks in the street. His head drops, he starts to notice less and less, begins to talk to himself, and finally stops in the middle of the street. The anonymity of the street, in spite of its many passers-by, allows Raskolnikov to indulge his flight from the realities of actual human contact.

Thus references to Dostoyevsky's personal situation as the root of his concern with doubles are not enough: as he has Svidrigaylov say, the streets of the administrative capital of Russia (a telling detail) are full of people talking to themselves. It is true that Dostoyevsky referred to *The Double* as a confession, and Stanley M. Coleman suggests that Golyadkin can be seen as a self-portrait:

There can be no doubt that the sudden change in [Dostoyevsky's] circumstances, resulting from instantaneous popularity, had turned the young author's head. *The Double* represents in an exaggerated manner his own bitter reflections at the foolish way in which he had behaved at that time. (Coleman 1934, 262)

But, as I have observed elsewhere about similar arguments concerning Kafka's portrayal of human alienation, if this were all Golyadkin and his double stood for then there would be little of interest for the reader with no curiosity about the author's personal experiences.

The theme of the double in Dostoyevsky's work always seems to raise large *social* issues for consideration. In his masterpiece, *The Brothers Karamazov*, the long monologues both of the Elder Zossima and of the Public Prosecutor make this palpably clear. As the former argues:

in our age all men are separated into self-contained units, everyone crawls away into his own hole, everyone separates himself from his neighbour, hides himself away and hides away everything he possesses, and ends up by keeping himself at a distance from people and keeping other people at a distance from him. He accumulates riches by himself and thinks how strong he is now and how secure, and does not realize, madman that he is, that the more he accumulates the more deeply does he sink into self-destroying impotence. For he is used to relying on himself alone and has separated himself as a self-contained unit from the whole. He has trained his mind not to believe in the help of other people, in men and mankind, and is in constant fear of losing his money and the rights he has won for himself. Everywhere today the mind of man has ceased, ironically, to understand that true security of the individual does not lie in isolated personal efforts but in general human solidarity. (Dostoyevsky 1958, 357)

We are back, I think, to the same two systems of values that we saw in *Love and Commitment*; the perspectives of exchange and those of solidarity. Golyadkin, ironically, is in one sense not a madman; he does not want to accumulate riches, he does not want to rely on himself alone, hiding himself away from others. He wishes to be respected and loved for himself as a real person, without a mask, without hypocrisy, and he does seek help from others. But he lives in a society in which it is only those who behave in the artificial manner of the double who are accepted, who do succeed.

If Dostoyevsky's entire *oeuvre* is permeated by a fascination with the complexities and contradictions of personality, his literary techniques for exploring this fascination change. Except on rare, dramatic occasions doubles are not introduced directly in his fiction after *The Double* (an example of such dramatic exceptions would be Ivan's hallucinated image of aspects of himself, personified as the devil, in *The Brothers Karamazov*). He uses, more often, characters who are either unusually revealing of their inner thoughts – eccentrics – or unusually reticent, to bring out into the open those conflicts which are often hidden within the 'normal' individual. Thus in his address to the reader in book one of *The Brothers Karamazov* he denies that an eccentric is an exception, and claims that sometimes, on the contrary, he 'expresses the very sum and substance of a certain period'. A few pages later, we are told of old Karamazov that he 'liked to dissemble, to play some unexpected part before you, sometimes moreover, without the slightest need for it'. Such characters are, as Dostoyevsky claims, unusual not so much because they are different from ordinary people, but because they reveal what is hidden in ordinary people. The artistic effect of *The Idiot* is dependent upon the veil-stripping effects of an individual who acts always in an open, human way, unmotivated by desire for personal gain.

In *Crime and Punishment* it is Mr Luzhin who expresses this dilemma that the individual hesitating between self-interest and solidarity is imprisoned in – although, of course, the whole novel explores the inability of man to live by pure self-interest alone.

'[. . .] If, say, I've been told in the past, "Love thy neighbour as thyself," and I did, what was the result of it? [. . .] 'The result of it was that I tore my coat in half to share it with my neighbour, and both of us were left half naked. As the Russian proverb has it, "If you run after two hares, you won't catch one." But science tells us, "Love yourself before everyone else, for everything in the world is based on self-interest. If you love only yourself, you'll transact your business as it ought to be transacted, and your coat will remain whole." And economic truth adds that the more successfully private business is run, and the more whole coats, as it were, there are, the more solid are the foundations of our social life and the greater is the general well-being of the people. [. . .]' (Dostoyevsky 1974, 167)

Milton Friedman's theories are, we may note in passing, hardly modern. Their implementation has led to about as much human happiness in the present day as it did in Dostoyevsky's time. Moreover, Dostoyevsky's work shows, time and time again, how impossible and contradictory an aim total self-interest is. The hero of *Notes from the Underground* is as incapable of maintaining his initial posture of universal selfishness in that work as is Raskolnikov. And again it is worth noting that his contradictory modes of behaviour to Liza coincide with contradictory social attitudes concerning human relationships and, in particular, the treatment of women. The brothel and the loving family circle are used to exemplify and symbolize these contradictory attitudes, but as the story reveals very tellingly, the contradictions exist within the consciousness and beliefs of the underground man as much as outside in society in institutions as different as the house of prostitution and the respectable private home. The long monologue which Golyadkin delivers while standing behind the pile of logs late on in *The Double* oscillates between the same two views of womanhood and male-female relationships as does the account of the underground man. Although he is ostensibly waiting for Clara Olsufyevna in order to elope with her, he is also conducting an imaginary conversation with her in which he pours scorn on the romantic illusions spread by French novels, and counsels obedience to parental authority.

Georg Lukács is perhaps best known today for the uncompromising nature of his critique of modernism, and to the extent that Dostoyevsky's work is prophetic of certain modernist developments it might be thought that Lukács would be critical of the Russian novelist. In fact Lukács deals with Dostoyevsky very sympathetically, and discusses his work in terms of its containing symptomatic evidence of the corrupting power of modern society. In particular, he sees in Dostoyevsky's work an element that Brecht was later to detect in the work of Kafka: a response to the alienating pressures of contemporary urban life. As he says,

Dostoyevsky was the first – and is still unsurpassed – in drawing the mental deformations that are brought about as a social necessity by life in a modern city. (Wellek 1962, 153)

The city is, for the first century or so of its modern existence as an accumulation of millions of people, a specifically capitalist phenomenon, and aspects of city life are, for most of the nineteenth century, inseparable from the particular nature of capitalist social relations. This is an important point, and needs to be remembered when we consider the treatment of the city in literature. Writers' fascination with the odd mixture of cooperation and privacy, of the social and the individualist, that is found in the city has to be seen in the context of their belonging to societies in which the relationship of the public with the private was generally problematic.

The city becomes increasingly crucial as context for the portrayal of shattered or divided personality in literature as the nineteenth century unfolds. The anonymity its paradoxically crowded streets provide gives the writer a suitable objective correlative for the depiction of that hidden, 'personal' side of his or her characters' personalities. At the same time, as we have already seen, that ability to indulge one's private fantasies and impulses in secret which the city provides, allows individuals to re-project their repressed selves back into the social world. That classic of Victorian pornography with its revealing title – *My Secret Life* – is set mainly in the towns and cities of late Victorian England, and especially London.

In my earlier chapter on multiple personality I made reference to the 'Strange Case of Silas Pronge', as Robert Howland Chase's title has it, who disappeared from his home at the age of 60 and was found in another town suffering from amnesia and running a shop under another name. In his account of the case Chase makes reference to Stevenson's *Dr Jekyll and Mr Hyde*, and it is true that Pronge's story does have a Jekyll and Hyde aspect to it. But it bears a much closer resemblance to another work of Victorian literature – Nathaniel Hawthorne's short story *Wakefield*. As does Pronge's case, *Wakefield* serves to illuminate for us the complex relationship between the anonymity provided by modern society, and the divisions and contradictions that its members internalize. In the case of Silas Pronge the size of the United States, and the existence of an efficient transport system are crucial factors. In the fictional account it is the anonymity provided within the modern, mass-population city that is central.

Hawthorne claimed that he had based the story on a newspaper report of a man living in London who absented himself for a long while from his wife.

The man, under pretence of going a journey, took lodgings in the next street to his own house, and there, unheard of by his wife or friends, and without the shadow of a reason for such self-banishment, dwelt upwards of 20 years. During that period, he beheld his home every day, and frequently the forlorn Mrs Wakefield [*his wife*]. And after so great a gap in his matrimonial felicity – when his death was reckoned certain, his estate settled, his name dismissed from memory, and his wife, long, long ago, resigned to her autumnal widowhood – he entered the door one evening, quietly, as from a day's absence, and became a loving spouse till death. (Hawthorne 1970, 164)

The story has the quality of myth, and like all myths it tells us something of the lives of those to whom the myth appeals. In part this is seen in the mixture of the familiar and the unfamiliar in the tale. There is nothing odd, in London, in knowing nothing about the person who lives a street away from you – indeed, many people know nothing of the person who lives next door to them. I say that there is nothing odd, by which I mean that there is nothing unusual; but of course there is something odd about this; millions of people, whose survival depends upon their mutual cooperation, are locked up in separate, non-communicating compartments.

Again, there is nothing odd in the simple sense about a wife not knowing too much about her husband's life outside the home. Many wives in modern societies hardly know what work their husbands do; it is important to note that the myth only works in the tale because it is the husband, not the wife, who extends that area of freedom and privacy he enjoys but which his wife does not to nearly the same extent.

Hawthorne suggests a link between the secret thoughts and selfish ideas of Wakefield and his mysterious absence. He notes of Wakefield's wife that without her

> having analyzed his character, [she] was partly aware of a quiet selfishness, that had rusted into his inactive mind; of a peculiar sort of vanity, the most uneasy attribute about him; of a disposition to craft which had seldom produced more positive effects than the keeping of petty secrets [. . .] (Hawthorne 1970, 165)

The mythical quality of the story comes from this bringing together of the anonymity of London's streets with the private, secret lives of its inhabitants – especially its male inhabitants.

But there are other suggestive elements in the story. Soon after his departure, Wakefield contents himself with the thought that his wife is, after all, only in the next street; but an authorial interjection denies this: 'Fool! it is in another world.' The similarity of this passage to one in De Quincey's *The Confessions of an English Opium Eater*, written some 20 years before *Wakefield*, is instructive. De Quincey had, revealingly, travelled from countryside to town prior to indulging himself with the altered states of consciousness achieved by means of opium (taken innocently at first, if we are to believe him). During poverty-stricken wandering through the streets of London he met a young prostitute, Ann, who was kind to him but with whom he lost contact. De Quincey claims to have searched for her, but without success.

If she lived, doubtless we must have been sometimes in search of each other, at the very same moment, through the mighty labyrinths of London; perhaps even within a few feet of each other – a barrier no wider, in a London street, often amounting in the end to a separation for eternity! (De Quincey 1908, 173)

What interests me here, in particular, is the repetitive idea of a search for human contact and solidarity which is frustrated by the anonymity of London. It is as if the geographical peculiarities and complexities of the city are made to stand for something deeper, some inability of this vast commercial network to satisfy its members' human needs and aspirations. Hawthorne tells of Wakefield that 'It was [his] unprecedented fate to retain his original share of human sympathies, and to be still involved in human interests, while he had lost his reciprocal influence on them' (Hawthorne 1970, 171). It does not seem too wayward an interpretation of the fascination this situation has for Hawthorne to see it as something not limited to such extreme situations as Wakefield's. In his extraordinary absence we see objectified a more common absence from controlling or reciprocal influence on 'human interests' suffered by millions of Wakefield's contemporaries in their daily lives.

To strike a more sombre note, it can be noted that the roots of the myth are still well-fed. Lukács, in his *The Meaning of Contemporary Realism*, took great exception to a comment in Musil's *The Man Without Qualities* in which Musil, referring to Moosbrugger, 'a mentally-retarded sexual pervert with homicidal tendencies,' suggested that if humanity were able to dream collectively it would dream Moosbrugger (Lukács 1963, 31). In one sense, of course, Lukács is correct to object to the negative and reactionary aspects of this statement. It universalizes a particular social decadence and – in the manner of much modernism – ignores its social and historical roots. Yet when this necessary context is added the statement is thought-provoking. During the year in which I am writing the trial of the so-called 'Yorkshire Ripper' has taken place in Britain. What has dominated much media coverage of this case – particularly in the time prior to an arrest having been made – has been the shocking idea that the man responsible might be leading a perfectly ordinary domestic life, surrounded by a loving family who knew nothing of his horrific exploits. 'It might be your next-door neighbour.' The fascination that such a case evokes seems to be related to the extent to which it is capable of revealing certain odd things about 'ordinary' life that habit and custom blind us to. One of these things is the wider issue of male violence to women, and an aspect of this is the relationship between the secrecies of male fantasy lives and the scope that the modern city gives for their indulgence.

If this seems rather a forced interpretation, consider the implications of the following case from 'real life', reported upon by Morton Prince in an essay which has recently been republished. The subject of the report was a young man of 22 years old, who according to Prince was 'essentially normal and responsible, of robust character and of decided intellectual ability' (Prince 1975, 197). Under hypnosis this young man revealed at least four distinct phases or moods, which Prince categorizes as follows: firstly the ordinary or quiet mood, very similar to his waking mood; secondly a 'gay mood' in which the man became hilarious and absurd, played practical jokes and was generally 'obstreperous and fantastic;' thirdly a 'malicious' mood in which he became 'a sort of "Jack the Ripper" ', exhibited a strong desire to inflict pain, asked permission to stab the experimenter and attempted surreptitiously so to do, and confessed to a wish to vivisect or, failing that, to strangle; and fourthly – not altogether surprisingly – a 'depressed mood'. I do not refer to this case to suggest that we are all Jack-the-Rippers manqué. On the other hand, as a reading of so many of Dostoyevsky's novels reveals, Prince's subject is not the only young man who is outwardly normal and responsible, of robust character and decided intellectual ability, who contains within himself violent and anti-social impulses.

One of the essential components of the mythic quality that the original Victorian Jack-the-Ripper's case possessed was the fact that he remained uncaught and anonymous, and it is significant that interest in his twentieth-century emulator lessened after his capture. When all was public, then the ability of the case to symbolize that underworld of repressed violence in society at large and in reflected form in the individual psyche was reduced.

If Silas Pronge's case leads us to think of Hawthorne's *Wakefield*, the horrific murders of a Jack-the-Ripper figure lead our thoughts back to *Dr Jekyll and Mr Hyde*, a story which Morton Prince suggests, literary exaggeration apart, 'is so true a picture of what is actually observed in cases of double personality that it can be used almost as well as an actual case from life' (Prince 1975, 201). Prince finds much significance too in the fact that Stevenson claimed to have based his story on a dream; according to Prince the dream was probably an allegorical working out of previous thoughts originating in personal mental conflicts. In support of this view Stevenson's own statement, quoted by Masao Myoshi in his book *The Divided Self*, that he had long been trying to write a story on this subject, 'to find a body, a vehicle, for that strong sense of man's double being which must at times come in upon and overwhelm the mind of every thinking creature' (Myoshi 1969, 294) is highly relevant. Myoshi, however, also makes some interesting comments on the text of *Dr Jekyll and Mr Hyde* itself:

> The important men of the book, then, are all unmarried, intellectually barren, emotionally stifled, joyless. Nor are things much different in the city as a whole. The more prosperous business people fix up their homes and shops, but in a fashion without chic. Houses give an appearance of 'coquetry', and store fronts invite one like 'rows of smiling saleswomen' (Chapter 1). The rather handsome town houses in the back streets of Dr Jekyll's neighborhood are rented out to all sorts – 'map-engravers, architects, shady lawyers, and the agents of obscure enterprises'

(Chapter 2). Everywhere the fog of the dismal city is inescapable, even creeping under the doors and through the window jambs (Chapter 5). The setting hides a wasteland behind that secure and relatively comfortable respectability of its inhabitants. (Myoshi 1969, 297)

As Myoshi's commentary suggests, Stevenson's classic study of dual consciousness can only be fully understood if it is seen not as a statement of the universal dualism of humankind, torn between good and evil (which is, admittedly, how Stevenson may have seen it), but as a work which arises out of the particular tensions and contradictions of Victorian society. Stevenson has Dr Jekyll himself talk of his recognition of 'the thorough and primitive duality of man', but an attentive reading of the book takes us not into the heart of an eternal truth about all human beings, but deeper and deeper into the specific contradictions of Victorian Britain.

The alternation of Jekyll and Hyde has much in common with the details of cases of multiple personality we have already looked at. The division serves, after its emergence, to solve problematic tensions for Jekyll:

[. . .] I saw that, of the two natures that contended in the field of my consciousness, even if I could rightly be said to be either, it was only because I was radically both; and from an early date, even before the course of my scientific discoveries had begun to suggest the most naked possibility of such a miracle, I had learned to dwell with pleasure, as a beloved daydream, on the thought of the separation of these elements. If each, I told myself, could but be housed in separate identities, life would be relieved of all that was unbearable; the unjust might go his way, delivered from the aspirations and remorse of his more upright twin; and the just could walk steadfastly and securely on his upward path, doing the good things in which he found his pleasure, and no longer exposed to disgrace and penitence by the hands of this extraneous evil. (Stevenson 1980, 49)

It is, surely, only in the context of a society in which the claims of self-interest and common humanity are in conflict that such a passage could be written.

In her undergraduate study of the theme of the double in Dostoyevsky's *The Double* and *The Brothers Karamazov* Sylvia Plath compares Smerdyakov and Ivan, from the latter work, with Hyde and Jekyll. She points out that Smerdyakov's growing confidence in Ivan's presence – like Hyde's increasing physical stature and strength – reflects the gradually maturing power of the evil Smerdyakov and the moral collapse of Ivan. She also draws attention to the fact that the crime of parricide, actually committed by Smerdyakov, with Ivan's tacit compliance, is symbolically attached to Hyde, who plays 'apelike tricks' on Jekyll, 'scrawling in my own hand blasphemies on the pages of my books, burning the letters and destroying the portrait of my father' (Plath 1955, 38). This behaviour also calls to mind that of Miss Beauchamp's different personalities, who carried their mutual antagonisms into the destruction of each others' property.

Hyde's name, of course, suggests the 'hidden' nature of the impulses he represents, and it is appropriate that the murder he commits should take place in the streets of London. London is the natural setting for *Dr Jekyll and Mr Hyde*, both because of its physical extensiveness and complexity and also because of the ethical and moral ambivalences which its Victorian expansion revealed and enacted. We cannot imagine this tale set in a quiet country village, or in a pre-industrial society; its links with nineteenth-century London are radical. Consider the resemblances between the following passage, and those quoted earlier from both Hawthorne and De Quincey:

> I was the first that could thus plod in the public eye with a load of genial respectability, and in a moment, like a schoolboy, strip off these lendings and spring headlong into the sea of liberty. But for me, in my inpenetrable mantle, the safety was complete. Think of it – I did not even exist! (Stevenson 1980, 52)

We are also, I think, given here some indication of the source of the fascination – morbid and horrific though it be – that the Jack-the-Ripper myth exercises upon the contemporary imagination.

The complex symbolism of the contemporary city, with its secrecies and compartmentalizations alongside its collectivities and its thronging 'public', needs to be remembered when we turn to consider the work of Dickens. For Dickens, the city – especially London – is no mere backdrop for his characters. It is the stuff from which they are constructed and from which they inherit their inner tensions and contradictions. Like Conrad, Virginia Woolf and Kafka – very different novelists admittedly, but with something in common with him – Dickens perceives necessary links between the nature of the contemporary city and the nature of the characters he depicts inhabiting it. Indeed, a comment of Brecht's concerning Kafka's work could well apply to Dickens's fiction. Brecht is here quoted by Walter Benjamin, who reports that what Kafka's *The Trial* conveyed above all to Brecht

> is a dread of the unending and irresistible growth of great cities. He claims to know the nightmare of this idea from his own intimate experience. Such cities are an expression of the boundless maze of indirect relationships, complex mutual dependencies and compartmentalizations into which human beings are forced by modern forms of living. (Bloch *et al.* 1977, 90)

Dickens, like Kafka, uses the city as a sort of metaphor for modern man. Its complexity is set against its compartmentalization; everything is connected, and everything is concealed. Indeed, we might say that for Dickens the *plot* of one of his novels is strikingly similar to the city in which it often unfolds; everything is, again, linked by iron laws of causal connection, but at the same time everything seems so unique, autonomous, free-standing: character, experience, personality.

I want now to spend some time talking about one novel of Dickens's – *Great Expectations*. There is a case to be made for *Great Expectations* as Dickens's finest novel: more tightly structured than many of its predecessors, more profound in its analysis of Victorian realities, less willing to escape into sentimentality or whimsy. Crucial to the novel is, again, the movement from country to city. Pip moves from a life in the countryside where experiences are above all direct and sensory rather than conceptual – the tickler, the fire, eating with Joe – to a life where such experiences are mediated through more complex sets of social relations, through more involved systems of value and significance. A fair example of this is the treatment of eating in the novel. Early on this represents one of Pip's central pleasures; eating silently, with Joe, each holding up their piece of bread to indicate, without the necessity for words, how ingestion was proceeding. Newly in London, Pip is schooled in the need to improve his table manners by the tolerant Herbert Pocket; the sensual is being overlaid by the conventional. Finally, when Magwitch returns and is given food in Pip's London rooms, Pip is disgusted by the animality of his eating. Pip is, at this stage, noticeably less tolerant of Magwitch than was Herbert of him.

Another sign of the increasing importance of *mediation* as Pip moves from the countryside to the town is the very acquisition of literacy. When we meet Pip on the first page of the novel he cannot pronounce his own name properly, and he reads more into the shape of the letters on his parents' tombstone than into their meaning. Even during the period of his greatest degeneracy in London, we learn that he sticks to his books, and while he is learning to speak correctly both Biddy and Joe are developing their command of language as well. Whereas Joe, early on in the novel, when asked by Pip how he spells 'Gargery' responds that he doesn't spell it at all, by the end of the novel both he and Biddy have acquired a certain level of literacy that makes both of them into more complex characters.

But this acquisition of literacy is two-sided. When Magwitch returns to see the 'gentleman' he has created – and the distorted echoes of *Frankenstein* are strong here – he insists on Pip's reading in a foreign tongue which he does not comprehend. Pleased with what he finds in Pip he exclaims

'[. . .] I says to myself, "If I ain't a gentleman, nor yet ain't got no learning, I'm the owner of such. All on you owns stocks and land; which on you owns a brought-up London gentleman?" [. . .]' (Dickens 1972, 339)

It is this corruption of a genuine extension of human ability – literacy – with the values of commercialism, that represents a central item of concern in *Great Expectations*. The fundamental paradox, surely, with which Dickens is battling in the novel is that the more an individual improves himself, the more he separates himself from others. It is a paradox for Dickens because he knows that history cannot be reversed and that the communality of pre-industrial, pre-urban society cannot be recaptured. And indeed, he knew from his own life that Pip's expectations were not contemptible: he had no desire to return to the blacking factory. But he perceives, too, the loss involved.

It is perhaps in the character of Wemmick that these tensions are presented most clearly, although I would argue that they are implicit through the book in Pip's own progress: the very ambiguity of the title of the work, with its hinting at the intertwining of commercial and human expectations indicates the direction of Dickens's concern. Wemmick's divisions are not at all arbitrary; the opposition between country and town is important here, but so too is that between the worlds of work and of leisure, of commercial relationships and family ones. When Pip visits Wemmick's home in the country – built like a castle – he asks him:

> 'Is it your own, Mr Wemmick?'
> 'O yes,' said Wemmick, 'I have got hold of it, a bit at a time. It's a freehold, by George!'
> 'Is it, indeed? I hope Mr Jaggers [*his employer, JH*] admires it?'
> 'Never seen it,' said Wemmick. 'Never heard of it. Never seen the Aged. Never heard of him. No; the office is one thing, and private life is another. When I go into the office, I leave the Castle behind me, and when I come into the Castle, I leave the office behind me. If it's not in any way disagreeable to you, you'll oblige me by doing the same. I don't wish it professionally spoken about.' (Dickens 1972, 231)

Wemmick is a man living by two opposed value-systems; his advice to Pip in London is based on the assumption that self-interest should predominate, but advising him on the same matter in the countryside he bases his response on the assumption that Magwitch is to be helped. Even so, there is, be it noted, a paradox in his London behaviour, for were it completely self-interested the invitation to Pip to seek further advice in the country would not be given. Even with Wemmick's geographical separation of solidarity and exchange, the former intrudes into the realm of the latter.

It seems clear that the conflict between enlightened self-interest and unselfish mutuality was inescapable for the Victorian writer trying to portray accurately the contending elements of single characters. In Mrs Gaskell's *North and South* Margaret Hale is struck by this same Wemmick-like contradiction in Thornton, the manufacturer, who is extremely kind to her and to her mother, but who defends a system which Margaret sees to be unfeeling and inhumane. We are told by Mrs Gaskell that 'Margaret's whole soul rose up against' Thornton while he reasoned 'as if commerce were everything and humanity nothing' (Gaskell 1979, 204), and at this point she can hardly thank him for the individual kindness which he has just displayed to her and her mother. Margaret perceives that he is aware that her mother is incurably ill;

> She saw it in his pitying eyes. She heard it in his grave and tremulous voice. How reconcile those eyes, that voice, with the hard, reasoning, dry, merciless way in which he laid down axioms of trade, and serenely followed them out to their full consequences? The discord jarred upon her inexpressibly. (Gaskell 1979, 205)

Margaret's solution to this jarring discord — and the solution is also, we feel, Elizabeth Gaskell's — is for there to be more direct personal contact between the social classes. She longs for Thornton and Higgins — the union leader — to speak together, 'as man to man', and for the latter to forget that Mr Thornton is a master, while the former listens with his human heart and not his master's ears. This urge for human reconciliation, symbolized at one point in the novel by the praying together of Higgins, Margaret and her father, is not so different from the later solution to social division advanced by E.M. Forster: 'only connect'. After his bankruptcy, and his consequent humbling, Thornton adopts this viewpoint, seeking to 'have the opportunity of cultivating some intercourse with the hands beyond the mere "cash nexus" ' (p. 525), and arguing the need to 'bring the individuals of the different classes into actual personal contact' (p. 525). The provision of money by Margaret allows this ideologically attractive compromise actually to take place.

In tension with this very unconvincing solution to class struggle in *North and South*, however, are a number of powerful passages in the novel which take a far more sombre view of the contradictions involved. Consider the following passage, which opens chapter 50 of the novel:

> Meanwhile at Milton the chimneys smoked, the ceaseless roar and mighty beat, and dizzying whirl of machinery, struggled and strove perpetually. Senseless and purposeless were wood and iron and steam in their endless labours; but the persistence of their monotonous work was rivalled in tireless endurance by the strong crowds, who, with sense and with purpose, were busy and restless in seeking after — What? In the streets there were few loiterers, — none walking for mere pleasure; every man's face was set in lines of eagerness or anxiety; news was sought for with fierce avidity; and men jostled each other aside in the Mart and in the Exchange, as they did in life, in the deep selfishness of competition. There was gloom over the town. Few came to buy, and those who did were looked at suspiciously by the sellers; for credit was insecure [. . .]. (Gaskell 1979, 510)

It seems clear that the tensions here are not going to be solved by personal contact between masters and men; quite apart from anything else, such contact is not going to bring new orders into the town.

In passages such as this I think that Mrs Gaskell avoids the fudging and blurring brought about by the ideological pressure for compromise. She sees here that there is no reconciliation to be found between the 'deep selfishness of competition' and the human needs of those enmeshed by the senselessness of the system. It is interesting that she fixes upon the behaviour of people in the street to symbolize their profounder social relationships, and her commentary upon their individualistic and selfish jostling of one another is prophetic of the view of the crowded street to be taken by so many modernist writers later on (and, at the same time, reminiscent of the same view of the street and its inhabitants in Blake's remarkable poem 'London').

In *Great Expectations* the anonymity of London is crucial to the divisions and complexities of individual characters. As Wemmick tells Pip when the latter wishes to conceal Magwitch, 'Under existing circumstances there is no place like a great city when you are once in it.' Wemmick's office – as important an element in his double life as Golyadkin's is to his – is in the heart of the city, and it deals with the most heartrending human problems in a purely business-like, cash-nexus manner. But Wemmick is not a bad man, and neither is Jaggers.

Waiting for Estella in London, having passed by the grim jail, Pip is struck by what he takes to be the utter contrast between her and the prison:

> While my mind was thus engaged, I thought of the beautiful young Estella, proud and refined, coming towards me, and I thought with absolute abhorrence of the contrast between the jail and her. (Dickens 1972, 284)

But the reader learns, in due course, that the proud and refined Estella is the daughter of the convict Magwitch, and this concealed connection between what appear to Pip to be two polar opposites is an apt reminder of the fact that Victorian society is a network of concealed connections, a mass of mediations joining – often very indirectly – people and institutions with apparently nothing in common. In one of the neatest illustrations of this Herbert Pocket tells Pip that although a gentleman may not keep a public house, a public house may keep a gentleman. Private property is an institution that gives the individual owner a double relationship to that owned; he or she is connected with the thing owned on one level, but separate from it on another.

One of the most oddly moving scenes in *Great Expectations* takes place late on in the book when Jaggers and Wemmick find out about each other's hidden selves.

> 'What's all this?' said Mr Jaggers. 'You with an old father, and you with pleasant and playful ways?'
> 'Well!' returned Wemmick. 'If I don't bring 'em here, what does it matter?'
> 'Pip,' said Mr Jaggers, laying his hand upon my arm, and smiling

openly, 'this man must be the most cunning imposter in all London.'
'Not a bit of it,' returned Wemmick, growing bolder and bolder. I think
you're another.'

Again they exchanged their former odd looks, each apparently still dis-
trustful that the other was taking him in. (Dickens 1972, 424)

Jaggers, for once, is doing something 'openly'; behaving like a human being
rather than a legal robot. But this genuine mutual pleasure at the discovery
of each other's humanity soon gives way to suspicion and concern. The 'odd
looks' are repeated several times,

with this difference now, that each of them seemed suspicious, not to say
conscious, of having shown himself in a weak and unprofessional light to
the other. (Dickens 1972, 426)

To re-establish their professional credentials they are unnecessarily unkind
to Mike, who makes the mistake of bringing his personal sorrows to their
attention. Business etiquette is thus made the mode of their office relationship once more.

In *Dr Jekyll and Mr Hyde* Stevenson has Jekyll utter a remark that links his
use of Hyde with the idea of a commercial relationship, by comparing the
way he summoned up Hyde with the behaviour of those who hire others to
do their dirty work for them:

Men have before hired bravos to transact their crimes, while their own
person and reputation sat under shelter. I was the first that ever did so for
his pleasures. (Stevenson 1980, 52)

The suggestion, surely, is that the Jekyll-Hyde division is no more marked
than the concealed contradictions allowed for by commercial relationships.
That outwardly respectable, upright citizen may be associated with some
very dubious goings-on through a financial interest, and were this associa-
tion to come to light – as it does in the case of Bulstrode, in George Eliot's
Middlemarch – then it is as if Dr Jekyll's door is burst open to reveal Mr
Hyde. Stevenson's mention of 'bravos' in the above quotation suggests
another interesting literary parallel, with the early nineteenth-century tale
The Bravo of Venice, which 'Monk' Lewis claimed to have translated from
the German. In this particular tale the theme of hiring someone else to do
your dirty work – a 'bravo' – is linked to a typical double-identity theme.
The novel is a poor one, full of clichés and predictabilities, but it is interesting how at this early date (1804) the double-identity theme whereby the
'respectable' Abellino becomes the 'bravo' Flodoardo to expose the corruption of Venetian society, is linked with the concealments and hypocrisies
made possible by money and commercial interest.

I have spoken as if the double-identity theme in *Great Expectations* were
associated only with commerce and with the city of London. But as a
number of critics have pointed out, Pip possesses a shadowy double in

the figure of Orlick before he sets off for London. Masao Myoshi suggests that

> Pip and Orlick are the symbolic representation of a personality divided in the classical Freudian sense. In fact, Pip's sexual passivity can only be adequately explained by Orlick's lecherous interest in Biddy and by his successor's (Drummle's) brutal beatings of Estella. In this use of doubling there is at least the tacit assumption that the psychological reality can no longer be contained within a single character but requires two or more for any adequate expression. (Myoshi 1969, 270)

Another possible explanation is that Dickens was unhappy in the portrayal of inner tensions and contradictions, and preferred to objectify these in the form of separate, opposed, but internally integrated characters. Even Wemmick, it may be noted, although divided is divided in a remarkably clean and uncluttered way. This predilection on Dickens's part may represent a tension in his own mind between his perception that human beings were divided by forces powerful in his society, and a desire to see these divisions overcome. Alternatively, we may note that objectifying human divisions in opposed but separate individuals rather than portraying them as internal tensions makes it easier to expose them in detail and to explore their ramifications.

Orlick represents Pip's darker impulses, perhaps, in ways other than are suggested by Myoshi. Almost everything he does can be seen as an expression of suppressed desires on the part of Pip. He strikes down Mrs Joe – after having verbally insulted her – he lusts after Biddy, he is drawn in apparent curiosity and fascination to Miss Havisham's place of self-imposed incarceration, and he stuffs Pumblechook's mouth full of bulbs! The nearest Dickens comes to any overt suggestion that the two represent forces in conflict within the individual rather than between individuals is in the final, rather unsuccessful melodramatic scene where Orlick announces that he is going to kill Pip. Thus what *Great Expectations* lacks is what Dostoyevsky portrays so well in his work: the revealed existence of contradictory impulses in the same individual struggling for mastery. The displacement of Pip's darker self into the figure of Orlick may have the effect of objectifying it and making it more apparent, but it tends to preclude a concern with more internalized individual conflict.

The treatment of Herbert Pocket in *Great Expectations* gives some evidence that Dickens shied away from the ultimate implications of certain of the contradictions he depicts in the novel. Early on in the text Pocket is presented in a way that suggests clearly that Dickens detected a clear incompatibility between his humanity and his chances of material and social success.

> Herbert Pocket had a frank and easy way with him that was very taking. I had never seen anyone then, and have never seen anyone since, who

more strongly expressed to me, in every look and tone, a natural incapacity to do anything secret and mean. There was something wonderfully hopeful about his general air, and something that at the same time whispered to me he would never be very successful or rich. (Dickens 1972, 201)

The thrust of this passage is towards a recognition of the incompatibility of openness and honesty, and success in Victorian Britain. But by the end of the novel Herbert – without being *very* successful or rich – is a successful enough businessman to undercut the force of this earlier description. It is not insignificant that his and Pip's success comes from work abroad, the implications of which in human terms – unlike the work of Jaggers and Wemmick – are never displayed. Here, as so often in the Victorian novel, we see the ideological retreat from the implications of what has been discovered. Just as Dickens qualifies his creative insight into the doomed nature of the 'old-fashioned' qualities of goodness portrayed early on in *Dombey and Son*, so too Mrs Gaskell retreats from the full implications of her insights in *North and South*, implying that perhaps a union of 'Southern' capital and 'Northern' business acumen, along with personal contacts between masters and hands, will resolve the incompatibilities between the human and the commercial that have previously been exposed. Such retreats make the ideological clarity of Charlotte Brontë's *Villette* – at which I now want to look – more impressive.

5

No Room of One's Own: Charlotte Brontë's *Villette*

I have now considered a number of cases in which divisions and contradictions within literary characters have been rendered unembarrassing through what could be called geographical and social compartmentalization. One thing that Dr Jekyll, Wakefield and Wemmick all have in common is that they live out their contradictory selves – as far as they possibly can – in separate environments. When this separation becomes difficult or impossible then serious problems ensue, as they did for Golyadkin, and as, briefly, they do for Jaggers and Wemmick. One other thing that all these characters have in common is their gender: they are all men. This is no chance coincidence, for it is men who have the geographical and social mobility at this time which allows them to effect such a neat separation between selves. It is not just the existence of the distinct worlds of the home and the office that gives men this freedom, but also the ability to enjoy the anonymity of the urban street in a way impossible for many women, especially middle-class women.

We would expect, then, that a crucial issue for a woman faced with inner divisions comparable to those experienced by the male characters we have considered would be that of finding a space – geographical and social – in which to exercise aspects of the self which cannot be given free rein within one set of social relationships. No literary work demonstrates this fact more clearly than Charlotte Brontë's *Villette*. In her last novel Charlotte Brontë explores the complex links between powerlessness, repression and self-division as they face the educated, poor, middle-class woman of her day. The obsessive concern for secrecy in the novel is directly related to the need for the powerless, educated woman to create an inner space in which to indulge repressed aspects of her personality, an inner space that performs the same function for a woman that the outer space of work, and town, performs for a man. As we will see, however, a woman's inner space involves far more constriction than does a man's more public way of indulging his second self.

Right from the start of *Villette* we are shown that contradictions have to be forced inwards, rather than thrust away outwards (to the West Indies, for instance, as in Paul's case), if you are a woman. Little Polly, facing the loss of the father she loves, has only one solution:

> The little creature, thus left unharassed, did for herself what none other could do – contended with an intolerable feeling; and, ere long, in some degree, repressed it. (Brontë 1981, 79)

Ten pages later, facing the loss of Graham Bretton, to whom she has transferred her affections, she reveals herself to Lucy Snowe, but she 'never showed my godmother one glimpse of her inner self' (p. 90). This juvenile repression of emotions is very reminiscent of the accounts given in many of our earlier case histories, and as I will argue later it is also important in considering the formation of 'Rochester's' character in Jean Rhys's *Wide Sargasso Sea*. Brontë, through a crude symbolism, identifies Polly with self-laceration and repression: as a child she is portrayed working a piece of cambric for Graham Bretton and marking it with the blood flowing from her pricked fingers; when she reappears in the novel, much later on, as a young lady she is wearing a white dress 'sprinkled slightly with drops of scarlet'. Along with self-laceration the theme of burial occupies a central symbolic role in the novel; the legend of the young nun buried alive because of her transgressions comes clearly to symbolize Lucy's view of her own fate, and, as an early comment directs us to understand, the fate of many *women and girls*.

> [. . .] I will permit the reader to picture me, for the next eight years, as a bark slumbering through halcyon weather, in a harbour still as glass – the steersman stretched on the little deck, his face up to heaven, his eyes closed: buried, if you will, in a long prayer. A great many women and girls are supposed to pass their lives something in that fashion; why not I with the rest? (Brontë 1981, 94)

When Lucy buries the letters which she has received from Graham Bretton, in the same garden in which the young nun was allegedly buried alive, she is attempting to do what Polly had done early on in the novel: to repress an intolerable hurt inwards. In both cases, be it noted, the hurt is caused by a man. When Graham Bretton himself suffers the pains of unrequited love no such repression is called for; he talks of his pain to Lucy, of all people!

Three of the characters of *Villette* are, in the course of the novel, described as divided individuals: Polly, Lucy Snowe and Graham Bretton. But what distinguishes the form of their division is that in the case of the two women it is a division between their public and private selves, whereas in the case of Graham Bretton it takes the form of two relatively distinct public selves.

Lucy, from early on in the novel, contrasts her outer and inner selves. Thus, after her having met Miss Marchmont for the first time, she examines herself in the mirror – a form of scrutiny much beloved by writers concerned with human doubles and divisions.

> I saw myself in the glass, in my mourning-dress, a faded, hollow-eyed vision. Yet I thought little of the wan spectacle. The blight, I believed, was chiefly external: I still felt life at life's sources. (Brontë 1981, 96)

Later on, as Lucy is observing the dome of St Paul's cathedral through her hotel window, on her first morning in London, the achievement of having escaped from her narrow life, of having been active rather than passive in the face of difficulties, encourages this concealed personality:

> While I looked, my inner self moved; my spirit shook its always-fettering wings half loose; I had a sudden feeling as if I, who had never yet truly lived, were at last about to taste life: in that morning my soul grew as fast as Jonah's gourd. (Brontë 1981, 108)

This is in London: later on in the town of Villette Lucy speaks of her soul re-entering the 'prison' of its 'poor frame'.

The effect of this division on both Polly and Lucy is to make them feel as if they are each two people. In Madame Beck's school, when she is given the chance to improve her status and become a fully-fledged teacher, Lucy admits that her unadventurous and unambitious character would, unless pushed, have let the chance slip – and adds:

> Besides, I seemed to hold two lives – the life of thought, and that of reality; and, provided the former was nourished with a sufficiency of the strange necromantic joys of fancy, the privileges of the latter might remain limited to daily bread, hourly work, and a roof of shelter. (Brontë 1981, 140)

There is an instructive parallel to be drawn between this comment, and a comment made by Virginia Woolf in her essay 'The New Biography':

> Truth of fact and truth of fiction are incompatible; yet he [*the biographer*] is now more than ever urged to combine them. For it would seem that the life which is increasingly real to us is the fictitious life; it dwells in the personality rather than in the act. (Woolf 1967, 234)

For a woman, be it again noted, 'reality' (Charlotte Brontë), or 'fact' (Virginia Woolf), are insubstantial and unsatisfying; what constitutes the fulfilling core of personal experience is thought or fiction, that which is inside, subjective, hidden; indulged in secret rather than acted upon. Virginia Woolf's use of the word 'fiction' reminds us, too, of an important link between the subjective and the process of literary composition – a link to which I shall return. Another, very similar quotation from Virginia Woolf – this time from her novel *Night and Day* – is strikingly reminiscent of the problematic situation of Lucy Snowe. In *Night and Day* Katharine Hilbery wonders why it is that there should be

> this perpetual disparity between the thought and the action, between the life of solitude and the life of society, this astonishing precipice on one side of which the soul was active and in broad daylight, on the other side of which it was contemplative and dark as night? (Woolf 1966, 358)

I said that I would return to the link between literary composition and subjectivity. The actual *form* of *Villette* bears important resemblances to inner dialogue – the sort of inner dialogue one does engage in when trying to tackle difficult problems that demand action, in an atmosphere of isolation and loneliness. It is true that at one point in *Villette* Lucy Snowe refers to the process of *writing* her story (p. 291), but it is as if her constructed Reader, to whom she addresses many comments, is an aspect of herself – just as, we feel, the writing of the novel was a form of self-scrutiny and inner dialogue to Charlotte Brontë. Very frequently in *Villette* we move from Lucy's indulgence in unexpressed thoughts to private self-examination, and from thence to dialogue with the personified 'Reader'. Thus on her return to Madame Beck's school after her collapse and recuperation with the Brettons we note the presence of a counterpointed sub-text in her farewell conversation with Graham:

> 'Lucy,' – stepping after me – 'shall you feel very solitary here?'
> 'At first I shall.'
> 'Well, my mother will soon call to see you; and, meantime, I'll tell you what I'll do. I'll write – just any cheerful nonsense that comes into my head – shall I?'
> 'Good, gallant heart!' thought I to myself; but I shook my head, smiling, and said, 'Never think of it: impose on yourself no such task. *You* write to *me*! – you'll not have time.' (Brontë 1981, 306)

Lucy's duplicity in this exchange is indicative neither of perversity nor shyness here; it is a necessary defensiveness, a form of behaviour that alone can guarantee her an independent identity. To reveal herself to Graham completely would be to abandon any independent self, to complement her social and economic dependence with an emotional dependence and to give herself into the hands of someone not concerned to possess her in that way.

Immediately after this passage, however, we move to a conversation between a personified 'Reason' and Lucy, concerning the likelihood of Graham's writing to her. The dialogue ends upon an inflexible and stern note:

> 'But if I feel, may I *never* express?'
> '*Never!*' declared Reason. (Brontë 1981, 307)

Expression there is, but not to another person; Lucy writes two separate letters to Graham in reply to his – one for her own relief, the other for his perusal (p. 334). As I have already pointed out, Lucy on one occasion informs the reader that she is *writing* her account: *Villette* is ostensibly her written, not her spoken or thought record. Our experience of the novel, then, puts us into the position of Lucy. By this I mean that only Lucy and the Reader are able to have knowledge both of Lucy's suppressed, private world and also of her public existence.

Talking about a similar example of inner dialogue in *Jane Eyre* Terry Eagleton refers rather scathingly to it as primarily a merely *literary* device:

> This brisk, unwittingly comic interior dialogue takes place between the

two facets of Jane: the meek, unworldly victim unable to act purposively, and the enterprising activist with an efficient knowledge of the measures essential for social advancement. That second Jane is repressed, depersonalized to a subconscious voice, sharply distinguished from the 'real' Jane who lacks the dynamism to succeed. The effect, then, is to show Jane moving eagerly forward without the objectionable implication that she is egoistically drafting her future. By the clumsy device of the divided self, Jane is able to make progress without detriment to her innocent passivity. (Eagleton 1975, 62)

This seems to me to be less than fair to Jane Eyre (and to Charlotte Brontë) and certainly capable of being extended to include a criticism too of Lucy Snowe, although this Eagleton does not attempt. To consider the divided self as a merely *literary* device is to fail to do justice to the extent to which Charlotte Brontë is concerned to demonstrate that a woman in the position of Jane Eyre or Lucy Snowe – educated, isolated and poor – *is* forced to be divided in a very fundamental way.

Introspective analysis suggests to me that internal dialogue takes place in ordinary human beings (the reader will have to accept my assurance that that is what I am) when one is isolated, with no one to talk to, and one needs to solve problems that demand action of one kind or another. We talk to solve problems; where we have no one apart from ourselves to talk to, then we talk to ourself. Whereas cerebration can on occasions be only marginally verbal, with enormous deletions and gaps in what we would consider appropriate to conventional speech, the solving of problems – especially those concerning human relationships – often brings forth a far more verbal train of thought. Where a literary character engages in inner dialogue it is a safe bet that he or she is isolated, with no one to talk to, and with problems to solve. In Joseph Conrad's *Under Western Eyes*, for instance, the student Razumov, forced to pretend to be a fellow revolutionary among Russian emigrés in Geneva on whom he has been ordered to spy, resorts to what Conrad's narrator describes as a silent thinking that is 'like a secret dialogue with himself' as well as to talking to himself in a diary. Leopold Bloom, in Joyce's *Ulysses*, in contrast, generally engages in an internal monologue; he is not considering *action* to solve his problems, and so the dialogue would represent an inappropriate form for his thoughts.

I think that there is an instructive parallel to be indicated between *Villette* and Jean Rhys's novel *Good Morning, Midnight*, which like Charlotte Brontë's novel depends considerably upon the tracing of the main character's inner dialogues. Sasha Jensen, Rhys's heroine, makes unspoken comments on the people she meets and talks to, and we can compare these with her actual utterances. But unlike the unspoken thoughts of, say, most of Virginia Woolf's characters, it becomes clear that Sasha Jensen's reactions and opinions have to be concealed because of her position of social and economic powerlessness. Take the following passage, in which Sasha

Jensen meets the English owner of the shop in which she is working in Paris:

> . . . He arrives. Bowler-hat, majestic trousers, oh-my-God expression, ha-ha eyes − I know him at once. He comes up the steps with Salvatini behind him, looking very worried. (Salvatini is the boss of our shop.) Don't let him notice me, don't let him look at me. Isn't there something you can do so that nobody looks at you or sees you? Of course, you must make your mind vacant, neutral − you are invisible.
> No use. He comes up to my table.
> 'Good morning, good morning, Miss—'
> 'Mrs Jensen,' Salvatini says.
> Shall I stand up or not stand up? Stand up, of course. I stand up.
> 'Good morning.'
> I smile at him.
> 'And how many languages do you speak?'
> He seems quite pleased. He smiles back at me. Affable, that's the word. I suppose that's why I think it's a joke.
> 'One,' I say, and go on smiling.
> Now, what's happened? . . . Oh, of course . . . .
> 'I understand French quite well. (Rhys 1969, 17; ellipses in original)

Sasha's inner dialogue, like Lucy's, is no mere technical device. It is what people resort to when they are isolated and powerless: particularly when they are powerless. Sasha's apprehensions are by no means idle: a few pages further on in the novel we learn that she has been dismissed by the owner. As she tells us much later on,

> Every word I say has chains round its ankles; every thought I think is weighted with heavy weights. Since I was born, hasn't every word I've said, every thought I've thought, everything I've done, been tied up, weighted, chained? And, mind you, I know that with all this I don't succeed. (Rhys 1969, 88)

The images of incarceration and enclosure in *Villette* come from the same source as Sasha's feeling of being chained up: isolation, poverty, and being female in a world of men.

Towards the end of *Good Morning, Midnight* Sasha makes this fear of other people quite explicit:

> 'You want to know what I'm afraid of? All right, I'll tell you. . . . I'm afraid of men − yes, I'm very much afraid of men. And I'm even more afraid of women. And I'm very much afraid of the whole bloody human race. . . . Afraid of them?' I say. 'Of course I'm afraid of them. Who wouldn't be afraid of a pack of damned hyenas?'
> Thinking: 'Oh, shut up. Stop it. What's the use?' But I can't stop. I go on raving. (Rhys 1969, 144, ellipses in original)

The passage enacts what it describes, as Sasha simultaneously describes her fear and also responds to it by complementing her public statements with concealed, inner address. The 'technical device' mirrors what people in Sasha's – and Lucy's – situation are forced actually to do: talk to themselves.

It is true that Graham Bretton is also portrayed as a divided, or 'doubled', person. But what is crucially different about his situation is that both 'selves' are displayed to other people, and they are complementary rather than contradictory; they each represent what he 'is' in two separate but related environments:

> The reader is requested to note a seeming [*N.B.! JH*] contradiction in the two views which have been given of Graham Bretton – the public and private – the out-door and the in-door view. In the first, the public, he is shown oblivious of self; as modest in the display of his energies, as earnest in their exercise. In the second, the fireside picture, there is expressed consciousness of what he has and what he is; pleasure in homage, some recklessness in exciting, some vanity in receiving the same. Both portraits are correct. (Brontë 1981, 273)

Graham has two 'spaces' in which to 'be'; he has the male privilege of a job and a home which are separate, but which involve no clash of interests for him, in spite of the fact that they allow him to display two different sides of his personality. For a woman, the case is different: both Polly and Lucy are divided as a direct result of Graham Bretton's influence. His presence renders Lucy mute, with him she lapses into near-silence:

> It was very seldom that I uttered more than monosyllables in Dr John's presence; he was the kind of person with whom I was likely ever to remain the neutral, passive thing he thought me. (Brontë 1981, 169)

'Dr John' is, of course, Graham Bretton; so described at this point in the novel before the fact that he is one and the same person that the reader has already encountered is revealed. But this other dual identity is, again, of no pain or consequence to him: a man can be divided with few problems, without even being aware of the fact. Lucy, however, as the above quotation makes clear, is unsexed in his presence, rendered neutral, turned into a 'thing'.

Much the same is done to Polly by Graham, and again a letter from him has a devastating effect. Polly tells Lucy that on receiving a letter from Graham avowing love, the letter

> lay in my lap during breakfast, looking up at me with an inexplicable meaning, making me feel myself a thing double-existent – a child to that dear papa, but no more a child to myself. (Brontë 1981, 464)

(It is interesting to compare this with Emily Brontë's description of Cathy, in *Wuthering Heights*, visiting the newly encountered Lintons and being led 'to adopt a double character without exactly intending to deceive any one' [Brontë 1975, 107]).

Once again the attention of a man turns a woman into a *thing*, and a divided thing. It is clear here that it is the contradictory view of women taken by men that divides women into two: Polly's two selves come about in precisely the same way that Kate Hardcastle's two selves are initially created: they are the constructions of man the father, and man the lover.

Not surprisingly, it is Lucy and not Graham whose identity becomes problematic for others: 'Who *are* you, Miss Snowe?' demands Ginevra Fanshaw, whose own identity is the uncontradictory construction of the men who desire her for her prettiness, wealth, and – we presume – ability to conform to what they want her to be. She is prepared to accept her identity as a gift from men; after all, although it is hardly her own, it is comfortable. But the self that Lucy is offered by Graham Bretton would, if accepted, be tantamount to suicide. For in spite of their divisions, Lucy and Polly have a sense of themselves as fundamentally unitary, as possessed of a real identity that is theirs and theirs alone, but which has to be masked in the world of men in which they live. Talking to Lucy of her childhood recollection of Graham, Polly says that he

'[. . .] was slighter than [*the mature Graham*], and not grown so tall, and had a smoother face, and longer and lighter hair, and spoke – not so deeply – more like a girl; but yet *he* is Graham, just as *I* am little Polly, or you are Lucy Snowe.'

I thought the same, but I wondered to find my thoughts hers: there are certain things in which we so rarely meet with our double that it seems a miracle when that chance befalls. (Brontë 1981, 361)

The passage is interesting from two angles. Firstly it demonstrates that aspects of the collective experience of women are, at this time, rarely experienced collectively, for the reason that they are repressed, privatized and considered to be unique. To this extent the very act of writing a novel such as *Villette* is a blow against the dehumanizing concealment of such common experience. But the passage also indicates that for women such as Polly and Lucy their private selves are in some ways more truly their own than are the public roles they are forced into. There is much concern with *acting* in *Villette* (Lucy is literally forced into a role by Paul Emanuel at one stage), and this is complemented by a repetitive set of references to *masks*. Again a comparison with Jean Rhys's *Good Morning, Midnight* is instructive. In this novel the heroine, like Lucy Snowe, is also forced into playing parts that inwardly she rejects, and again the effect upon her is to make her feel that her public self is a falsehood. Noticing that alcohol is breaking her face up, she comforts herself:

Besides, it isn't my face, this tortured and tormented mask. I can take it off whenever I like and hang it up on a nail. (Rhys 1969, 37)

Later on in the novel this feeling of unreality has spread to all public life, her description of which is uncannily similar to Lucy's of the evening celebration at the close of *Villette*:

> At this moment [*when she has told her escort that she has not eaten for three weeks JH*] a taxi draws up. Without a word he gets into it, bangs the door and drives off, leaving me standing there on the pavement.
>
> And did I mind? Not at all, not at all. If you think I minded, then you've never lived like that, plunged in a dream, when all the faces are masks and only the trees are alive and you can almost see the strings that are pulling the puppets. (Rhys 1969, 75)

Unfortunately, as R.D. Laing points out in *The Divided Self*, the person who does not act in reality but only in fantasy, becomes himself (or herself) unreal, and many of the case-histories he cites show that the creation of a false-self – a 'mask' – carries with it serious dangers, as the false self becomes more and more autonomous and extensive, and all that belongs to it becomes more and more dead, unreal, false and mechanical (Laing 1965, 143). Once this process is under way, the dangers of the individual's sinking into an overtly suicidal condition are considerable.

Bearing all this in mind it is not surprising that a key issue for a woman such as Lucy is the obtaining of enough private space to enable her to find and maintain her self, her human integrity. Like Virginia Woolf she requires a room of her own as well as the economic independence symbolized by the latter's £500 a year. In default of a physical space – the space that is spied upon and invaded by Madame Beck and her minions – the space must needs be inner space. It is for this reason that Lucy prizes and guards her own counsel, and rejoices to learn that her own secrecy is undisturbed:

> Who wills, may keep his own counsel – be his own secret's sovereign. In the course of that day, proof met me on proof, not only that the cause of my present sorrow was unguessed, but that my whole inner life for the last six months, was still mine only. (Brontë 1981, 545)

It is in this context that the significance of the two religious persuasions – Catholicism and Protestantism – is to be sought. Terry Eagleton is wrong, I think, to see the main thrust of opposition to Catholicism in *Villette* in terms of a 'healthy, rational, Protestant contempt for its lurid superstition and primitive otherworldliness' (Eagleton 1975, 67). The more significant objection, surely, is that Catholicism will allow Lucy – or anyone – no private space. The domain of Madame Beck, for Lucy, is permeated with a Catholic disregard for individual conscience (and conciousness):

> This was a strange house, where no corner was sacred from intrusion, where not a tear could be shed, nor a thought pondered, but a spy was at hand to note and to divine. (Brontë 1981, 310)

Protestantism, in contrast, as Paul Emanuel recognizes, allows for such privacy: he tells Lucy

> 'It is your religion — your strange, self-reliant, invulnerable creed, whose influence seems to clothe you in, I know not what, unblessed panoply. (Brontë 1981, 512)

Again, it is through an understanding of the significance of Catholicism to Lucy that we can move to an understanding of her attitude to Paul; it is when he grants her her private space (the school which will give her social and economic identity and independence) that she ceases to resist him. This also explains why he becomes less important to her as a lover, indeed, why his death is implied in an ending that seems deliberately designed to destroy the narrative illusion and to face the reader with Charlotte Brontë herself, pulling the strings of her puppets. Paul has granted Lucy selfhood, and thus his continued existence is no longer a matter of crucial importance to her. Charlotte Brontë seems determined to end the novel by saying, 'This woman has won the right to her own identity' rather than by implying that Lucy has found her true self in a man. Crucial to an understanding of the relationship between Paul and Lucy is a perception of its development from a male assault on female independence through to a male acceptance of female independence. Paul moves from saying that Lucy is 'one of those beings who must be *kept down*' (p. 226), to his offer not of love, but, significantly, of friendship. Paradoxically his calling her 'sister' is profoundly important, as this suggests a relationship based on equality.

> 'Why were you so glad to be friends with M. Paul?' asks the reader. 'Had he not long been a friend to you? Had he not given proof on proof of a certain partiality in his feelings?'
> Yes, he had; but still I liked to hear him say so earnestly — that he was my close, true friend; I liked his modest doubts, his tender deference — that trust which longed to rest, and was grateful when taught how. He had called me 'sister'. It was well. Yes; he might call me what he pleased, so long as he confided in me. I was willing to be his sister, on condition that he did not invite me to fill that relation to some future wife of his [. . .]. (Brontë 1981, 503)

Lucy's feelings, as expressed here, are complex. What is clear, however, is that the most important thing for her so far as her relationship with Paul is concerned is not that they should marry or achieve a sexual connection but that *deference* to each others' rights and individuality should be complemented by a certain exclusiveness and sharing of each others' confidences. To put it another way, Paul exchanges a part of his public life for part of Lucy's private life. Her internality is allowed to flow into his knowledge — so long as it goes no further. The self — the real, inner self — is not strong enough in Lucy's case to survive such exposure.

Charlotte Brontë's reported determination to end *Villette* with the strong implication that Paul Emanuel has been drowned seems to me to indicate the strength of her perception that any other ending would involve an element of ideological fudging or compromise. Paul has to die because Charlotte Brontë recognizes that for a woman such as Lucy the maintenance of a separate identity would not be possible within a marriage relationship with Paul. The ambiguity surrounding his implied death reminds us of the influence of her reading public, and of the extent to which such an ending would have been seen to constitute too overt an ideological assault upon Victorian assumptions.

6

Isolation and Identity: Joseph Conrad's *The Secret Sharer*

On my right hand there were lines of fishing-stakes resembling a mysterious system of half-submerged bamboo fences, incomprehensible in its division of the domain of tropical fishes, and crazy of aspect as if abandoned for ever by some nomad tribe of fishermen now gone to the other end of the ocean; for there was no sign of human habitation as far as the eye could reach. To the left a group of barren islets, suggesting ruins of stone walls, towers, and blockhouses, had its foundations set in a blue sea that itself looked solid, so still and stable did it lie below my feet; even the track of light from the westering sun shone smoothly, without that animated glitter which tells of an imperceptible ripple. And when I turned my head to take a parting glance at the tug which had just left us anchored outside the bar, I saw the straight line of the flat shore joined to the stable sea, edge to edge, with a perfect and unmarked closeness, in one levelled floor half brown, half blue under the enormous dome of the sky. (Conrad 1966, 91)

The opening lines of Conrad's *The Secret Sharer* are, it seems to me, crucial in any investigation into the meaning of this classic study of a double – or perhaps split – self. The story opens, it should be stressed, with the bemusement of the English sailor in the face of a colonized culture which he does not understand. Words like 'mysterious', 'incomprehensible' and 'crazy' in the first sentence of the tale fix the viewpoint very specifically. We do not – surely cannot – assume that the fishing stakes so described are incomprehensible or mysterious to those who put them there; nor can we believe that there really are no people living nearabouts who are responsible for the structures. The unnamed narrator of the story is, rather, the centre of this incomprehension, and it is an incomprehension based upon his separation from the culture which has produced the sights that puzzle him so.

We need to remember that this mysterious and incomprehensible environment constitutes the 'outer context' of *The Secret Sharer*. From an early point in the tale onwards attention is concentrated upon the Captain's isolation within his ship, but we need always to remember that this relatively local isolation takes place within the larger lonelinesses of imperialism. The description of sea, shore and sky which follows the opening sentences has the effect of fixing a number of interrelated forms of alienation for the reader; it is as if the narrator of the story can feel (at this stage) part of a purely natural, not social universe. No familiar cultural landmarks remind him of his membership of any group or collective body of human beings; he is a stranger in a ship full of cultural interlopers.

In some ways we can see the ship with its newly arrived captain as a parallel to the colonial culture it is leaving. In both cases a stranger wielding power has arrived to control an already established community, and the opening page of the tale leads the reader to see the young Captain as representative, on one level, of the European colonist arriving to 'lead' a foreign community. Conrad very often relates power and isolation, and particularly so when he is dealing with the colonial or imperialist context, as works such as *Heart of Darkness* and *An Outpost of Progress* demonstrate. And there seems to me to be a clear link between power, isolation, excessive self-consciousness, and the appearance of a double in *The Secret Sharer*.

Isolation breeds self-consciousness – both for individuals and for whole communities. If you have no one to talk to, then to stay sane you talk to yourself. Stranded amongst people you do not know, your awkwardness and self-consciousness remind you of aspects of yourself which, in easy communion with others, you forget. And in addition to this, your self-consciousness reminds you of your power to choose different forms of behaviour: you can picture different possible ways of relating to those from whom you feel, at present, isolated – and thus you can picture your own different potential selves. This is the situation in which the young Captain of *The Secret Sharer* finds himself.

Isolation divides the self in a very simple way, because in solitude you almost inevitably start thinking of the various different selves you could be, whereas the unselfconscious individual, acting with others in a common task, forgets him or herself. He or she becomes single in action, with an attention directed outwards, feeling more perceiver than perceived. In isolation one is conscious of being perceived rather than perceiving, and consequently one perceives oneself, one is split between perceiving and perceived self. We experience this whether we are the odd one out at a party or a foreigner abroad, when the everyday assumptions about ourselves become problematic, become the arena of choice about the identity we wish to present to others. We then recognize two selves: the self we have lived without being aware of it, and the self we see others scrutinizing. We see then that our identity is something made rather than given, and we realize that this making can take different forms between which we must choose.

The narrator of *The Secret Sharer* feels that both he and his ship are forced into this consciousness of themselves.

> In this breathless pause at the threshold of a long passage we seemed to be measuring our fitness for a long and arduous enterprise, the appointed task of both our existences to be carried out, far from all human eyes, with only sky and sea for spectators and for judges. (Conrad 1966, 92)

Thus, as with the subjects of many of our initial case-histories, his experience of something akin to double personality is preceded by considerable strain and isolation.

> It must be said [. . .] that I knew very little of my officers. In consequence of certain events of no particular significance, except to myself, I had been appointed to the command only a fortnight before. Neither did I know much of the hands forward. All these people had been together for eighteen months or so, and my position was that of the only stranger on board. I mention this because it has some bearing on what is to follow. But what I felt most was my being a stranger to the ship; and if all the truth must be told, I was somewhat of a stranger to myself. The youngest man on board (barring the second mate), and untried as yet by a position of the fullest responsibility, I was willing to take the adequacy of the others for granted. They had simply to be equal to their tasks; but I wondered how far I should turn out faithful to that ideal conception of one's own personality every man sets up for himself secretly. (Conrad 1966, 93)

What this passage reveals, importantly, is that like Golyadkin, the narrator feels divided *before* the appearance of his 'double'. The use of the word 'secretly' in the last sentence quoted above should alert us: the narrator has a 'secret sharer' before Leggatt appears – the secret 'ideal conception of one's own personality' that his self-consciousness has produced in the sort of situation which is almost inevitably productive of such conceptions: in isolation prior to a test of one's personal ability and worth. Few people can have been untouched by this sort of experience at comparable times – before an important examination for example.

Robert Rogers, in his *The Double in Literature* (1970) makes some interesting points about the 'summoning up' of the double, Leggatt, by the Captain. He points out that in various ways the two characters reflect the contradictions that have been seen in Conrad himself by his biographers – between loyalty and rebellion, patriotism and exile, maturity and youth, order and passion, realism and idealism, and so on. Rogers refers, too, to Guerard's suggestion that in being responsible for a ladder dangling over the side of the ship the Captain has 'symbolically summoned his double', and he notes that it is appropriate that the double should be summoned at this particular stage of the Captain's career when he is starting his first command and feels insecure about his role (Rogers 1970, 43).

Is Leggatt, then, merely a phantom produced by the narrator's isolation and strain? To the best of my knowledge no critic has suggested this, and unlike *The Double, The Secret Sharer* does not seem to encourage this reading. It is, however, an interesting exercise (for reasons upon which I will expand later) to see to what extent it is possible to read the tale as an account of hallucination. During the course of the tale no one else actually sees Leggatt, although we are told that the steward hears him moving about, and on one occasion it may be that he is mistaken for the Captain. His only real contact is with the narrator. It is true that the narrator tells us about Leggatt before the captain of the *Sephora* comes aboard to announce the missing man, but then the narrator is himself responsible for the order in which he tells us his story. Certainly Conrad insistently uses phrases like 'secret self' and 'second self' throughout the tale. Furthermore, the similarities between the two characters are stressed: both are Conway boys, both are young and both have to contend with failures of nerve on the part of fellow officers (the mate despairs as the ship nears land in exactly the same way that Archbold despaired in the storm). Moreover, some of the comments of the narrator's concerning Leggatt seem almost deliberately ambiguous in their possible reference to the Captain himself:

> At breakfast time, eating nothing myself, I presided with such frigid dignity that the two mates were only too glad to escape from the cabin as soon as decency permitted; and all the time the dual working of my mind distracted me almost to the point of insanity. I was constantly watching myself, my secret self, as dependent on my actions as my own personality, sleeping in that bed, behind that door which faced me as I sat at the head of the table. It was very much like being mad, only it was worse because one was aware of it. (Conrad 1966, 113)

It seems impossible to escape the conclusion after reading passages like this that if Conrad did not want to raise the suspicion that Leggatt was a creation of the narrator's imagination (the 'legate', the ideal conception of himself), then he wished to inspire the reader to associate him directly with the inner self, as yet untried, of the young Captain. At one point the narrator actually asks, rhetorically, 'Can it be [. . .] that he is not visible to other eyes than mine?' (Conrad 1966, 130).

Certainly the tale of Leggatt's sums up the Captain's own secret fears: the dream-like feel of the tale comes from its objectifying fears which, in waking life, are repressed and concealed even from the self. Archbold's statement to Leggatt touches upon the central preoccupation of the Captain – his own ability to rise to a new set of demands: 'Mr Leggatt, you have killed a man. You can act no longer as chief mate of this ship.' When Archbold comes aboard the other's ship, the Captain is made to feel

> as if I, personally, were being given to understand that I, too, was not the sort that would have done for the chief mate of a ship like the *Sephora*. I had no doubt of it in my mind. (Conrad 1966, 119)

As various commentators on the tale have pointed out, Leggatt is throughout associated with sleep and the unconscious. He appears naked issuing 'a faint flash of phosphorescent light', and is clad, and remains clad, in the captain's sleeping suit. At the end of the tale, after he has left the ship, the Captain, prior to catching sight of the hat he has given Leggatt, complains that

I could see nothing except a faint phosphorescent flash revealing the glassy smoothness of the sleeping surface. (Conrad 1966, 142)

The repetition is instructive; it suggests that the sea symbolizes the dividing line between sleep and awakening and that, as Joan E. Steiner has argued,

the lowering of Leggatt into the water and passing 'out of sight into unchartered regions' suggests the resubmergence of the captain's unconscious and the reintegration of his personality. (Steiner 1980, 183)

As Leggatt remarks wryly to the Captain, 'As I came at night so I shall go'.
More strikingly even, perhaps, Leggatt resembles Golyadkin's double in at least one sense as,

haggard as he appeared, he looked always perfectly self-controlled, more than calm – almost invulnerable. (Conrad 1966, 127)

And, finally his disappearance coincides with the Captain's achieving mastery over the ship; as his ideal conception of himself emerges into reality to display the qualities of control and command he has imagined for himself, his double disappears.
I said that in one sense Leggatt resembled Golyadkin's double – in his self-control and apparent invulnerability. And yet of course we know that he has lost his self-control on one occasion and is by no means invulnerable. He has killed a man. To this extent it is possible to argue that he represents the polar possibilities which await the Captain in the course of his first command: success or failure.

'Be careful,' he murmured, warningly – and I realized suddenly that all my future, the only future for which I was fit, would perhaps go irretrievably to pieces in any mishap to my first command. (Conrad 1966, 135)

Leggatt, at this point, could easily represent the Captain's personified fears and hopes: fears of one fatal mistake, hopes for the crucial decisive action under stress – and awareness of the thin partitions between the two.
To read *The Secret Sharer* as the account of a hallucination requires some straining of the evidence, but much less than at first sight might appear to be required. There is, too, the interesting evidence that Conrad interrupted the writing of *Under Western Eyes* to compose *The Secret Sharer*, and Conrad suffered a major breakdown after completing the larger work, a breakdown which included a series of hallucinated encounters with characters from the novel. I should say that I do not think that Conrad meant the reader to read *The Secret Sharer* as if Leggatt were purely a figment of the narrator's imagination. The fact that such a reading appears less strained than might have been thought to have been the case suggests, however, that Conrad was perhaps interested in using Leggatt as an objectification of the Captain's inner fears.

The Secret Sharer certainly explores ideas which are dealt with also in *Under Western Eyes* and in others of Conrad's novels. The Captain's isolation, and the resultant splitting of his personality and threat of insanity are very reminiscent of the similar results of Razumov's isolation as a secret agent for Czarist Russia amongst Russian emigrés in Geneva. And that, too, reminds us that the theme of secrecy and its effect on the integrity of the personality is dealt with elsewhere by Conrad – particularly in *The Secret Agent* and in *Lord Jim*. Indeed, Leggatt's appeal to the Captain, and the latter's feeling that 'a mysterious communication was established already between us two', are strongly reminiscent of the appeal Gentleman Brown makes to Jim in *Lord Jim*, a novel also much preoccupied with the lasting effects of a momentary lapse (and a lapse, be it noted, on the part of an English Second Mate who comes originally from a Parsonage).

I have already pointed out that Razumov, in his isolation in Geneva, also talks to himself a lot, and one could argue, too, that the divisions of Adolf Verloc's life, in *The Secret Agent*, are (literally and metaphorically) finally brought home to him. Joan E. Steiner points out that Conrad refers to E.T.A. Hoffmann in the course of *Under Western Eyes*, and that *The Secret Sharer* bears many points of similarity to Hoffmann's use of the theme of the double. Hoffmann, incidentally, seems to have lived something of a double life himself; spending his nights drinking with friends, writing in the early morning, then going off to his respectable job. Conrad certainly uses Leggatt to represent that sense of a second self that is conjured up in the narrator by his isolated and demanding situation. He even, I think, drops certain hints that Leggatt might be in part the creation of the Captain's fantasizing. What is significant is that once again we find that the double emerges in response to – or alongside – serious pressures on the individual who experiences the double. The source of duality – as in our case histories earlier on, and also, it may be added, as in *The Secret Agent* and *Under Western Eyes* – is not inside the individual but outside.

> And now I forgot the secret stranger ready to depart, and remembered only that I was a total stranger to the ship. I did not know her. Would she do it? How was she to be handled? (Conrad 1966, 141)

At the moment the external pressure is lifted – the Captain assures himself of his control over the ship – the secret stranger is forgotten, and departs. Would not Golyadkin's double have disappeared had he been able to resolve the social and sexual crises which, in the event, destroyed him?

It is also at the moment that the ship leaves the colonial context, with its 'mystery' and 'incomprehensibility' that the Captain's secret sharer swims away. Moreover, as this happens the Captain starts to *work*; he chooses one of the possible selves he has had the potentiality to become, and in doing so he irrevocably dismisses the others from the realm of the possible. In idleness he is haunted by an image of what he can become in the shape of

Leggatt; in activity alongside other human beings this threatening phantom disappears. Cutler and Reed (1975), concluding their single case-study of multiple personality, note that their findings confirm Janet's suggestion that with multiple personality there is a tendency towards remission with the passage of time. They add the final comment that

> In the case described, remission was associated in the patient's view with the alleviation and passing of psychological stresses, and this would suggest that effective therapy should be aimed at discovering and removing the stresses that originally precipitated the fugue. (Cutler and Reed 1975, 25)

Conrad's artistic insight seems to have arrived at a comparable conclusion: we are haunted by our own doubles when we are under pressure to be a person that we have no evidence we can become, but when we are what we want to be the secret sharer vanishes.

Conrad's Captain is able to sail away from the land where he is an alien, surrounded by incomprehensible and mysterious sights and experiences. And the community to which he belongs on ship is an ordered, integrated and unsecretive one where all are united in a variety of collective tasks. What of those unable to sail away – those condemned to remain in a divided and hostile environment? It is to the fate of such as these that I would now like to turn.

7
Race, Relationship and Identity: William Faulkner and Jean Rhys

> Mühlmann pointed to the fact that spirits that possessed an individual in a conquered country tended to speak in the language of the oppressor. (Ellenberger 1970, 190)

Consider the following plot-summary of a novel: 'A man marries a woman in the West Indies, where she is living but where he is a member of a foreign (but powerful) authority. He has already had certain forms of individualistic behaviour instilled in him from his childhood onwards, and this has turned him into a 'loner', a person who does not willingly reveal publicly his innermost emotions or feelings – or his ultimate ambitions. He is desperately in search of wealth. He puts aside his wife when he discovers the existence (as he thinks) of something unexpected in her, something which he believes her to have inherited from her family, and which he accuses her of having hidden from him. He leaves the West Indies and returns to his native country. She also comes to this country, but her presence and her relationship with him are kept secret. The wife has experienced racial hostility in the West Indies, where she has been considered a racial outsider, and this hostility has culminated in an uprising and the dramatic firing of a house. The man remarries and his second wife is ignorant of the existence of her predecessor, but this second marriage is blighted by the influence of the former relationship. The story ends with another fire, reminiscent of the former conflagration, which in complex ways "undoes" the earlier tensions and contradictions associated with the first relationship.'

If the plot seems familiar this is not surprising, as it is the plot of both William Faulkner's *Absalom, Absalom!* and Jean Rhys's *Wide Sargasso Sea*. It is also of course closely related to the plot of Charlotte Brontë's *Jane Eyre*, out of which *Wide Sargasso Sea* emerged. Much more could probably be written about Charlotte Brontë's novel, but in this chapter I want to concentrate on the two later works.

There are of course some differences of substance between the two novels; in Faulkner's work Henry Sutpen has come originally from the slave-owning south of the United States, to which he returns after making his money in the West Indies. In *Wide Sargasso Sea* the man (who we assume is Rochester from *Jane Eyre*, and who I will for convenience refer to as such although he is not named in the novel) has come from England, and he also

91

returns to his mother country after making – or, rather, marrying – his fortune in the West Indies. The difference is not so crucial as it might seem, for although the United States is not directly involved in the exploitation of slaves in the West Indies in the way that Britain is in Rhys's novel, it does at the time Sutpen returns home have slaves of its own who, being the same colour as those in the West Indies, indicate symbolically the same sort of link of guilt between the two countries that exists in a more directly political way in *Wide Sargasso Sea*.

Both novels, I would argue, offer fascinating accounts of the ways in which larger conflicts between societies and races generate internal contradictions in their members, contradictions which can no longer be balanced in the manner of Dickens's Wemmick, and which thus threaten the unity and integrity of the characters concerned. In *Absalom, Absalom!* the process whereby larger contradictions and repressions are absorbed into the very heart and substance of individual characters is carried over a number of generations, and is strikingly symbolized in the results of miscegenation; the sexual exploitation of black women by white men stands for a much more comprehensive exploitation of black by white, and the mixed-race children who result from such exploitative unions suggest both the internalization in later generations of the external conflicts and repressions of earlier generations, and also the inability of the white exploiters to escape the evidence of their earlier corruption. In very general terms, we can say that the 'finding out' of Sutpen by his mixed-race son Bon represents, in turn, both the inability of the individual to escape from the human origins of his or her social position, and also the 'return of the repressed', in Freudian terminology; the re-emergence into the public of previous public ills that have been hidden in the individual (Bon can pass for white).

I have mentioned the Freudian concept of repression, and with a novel like *Absalom, Absalom!* it seems difficult to ignore the fact that, as John T. Irwin notes in his study of Faulkner, although Faulkner denied the influence of Freud, repetitive patterns in his novels are so open to Freudian interpretations that some consideration of them from this point of view seems worth while. But I would distinguish my own approach to the novel from Irwin's in a crucial sense: whereas he tends to see the heart of the novel to reside in Faulkner's presentation of archetypal repressions and relationships within the family, a presentation which is set in and sometimes objectified through the history of the slave-owning South, my own interpretation would reverse this hierarchy of meaning. For me the novel expresses not universal human truths concerning the relationships between parents and children, brothers and sisters, and so on, but the particular crises in human relationships within and outside the family which are the product of a very specific set of social conflicts and repressions. In order to express the connection between these crises and their social and historical causation Faulkner makes use of mythic and archetypal references and frameworks, as the very title of the novel suggests, but this does not justify our seeing the tensions of *Absalom,*

Absalom! to be the universal experiences of all human beings. The trouble with many Freudian or semi-Freudian approaches to repression and conflict is that they tend to reject the historical explanation in favour of explanations based on universal family tensions which are presumed to exist for all times and all places. But as I have already argued, the family is by no means a historically stable institution, and we do Faulkner's penetrating social insight no justice if we assume that it is.

It is clear, of course, that the theme of incest is central to Faulkner's creative imagination, and that the desired but unconsummated sexual union between Quentin Compson and his sister Caddie – which the reader has learned of in Faulkner's previous novel *The Sound and the Fury*, in which events chronologically subsequent to those narrated in *Absalom, Absalom!* are recounted – constitutes a central source of Quentin's inner turmoil. It also symbolizes larger corruptions and sterilities within both novels. And as Masao Myoshi has pointed out, as the incestuous relationship dissolves the usual familial and extrafamilial bonds between individuals it 'finally dissolves the identifying masks distinguishing one individual from another', and thus serves to fix the incestuous act as 'the moment for the self meeting with itself' (Myoshi 1969, 11). But it is important to look at the specific context of the incest theme in Faulkner's work, and to resist the temptation to see it in purely archetypal and ahistorical terms. Irwin's Freudian approach to the novels leads him to imply that it is because incest signifies a recurrent and universal form of human generational conflict that in Faulkner's novels it can, along with other corrupted and distorted familial relationships, gather to itself a peculiar strength and representativeness. My own feeling is that it is only in consort with more specific social and historical conflicts and repressions which are both contained in and represented by these domestic tensions and perversions that incest achieves the force that it does achieve in a novel such as *Absalom, Absalom!*. In Faulkner's novel the theme of incest and the references to Oedipal tensions have to be examined alongside other corruptions of human sexuality and love resulting from the misuse of force, and the turning in upon itself of the human race to exploit and persecute part of itself – in brief, the Southern exploitation of black slaves. To be sure, Irwin mentions these issues, but it is not clear that he sees them to be the primary factors in the formation of repressed and doubled characters in *Absalom, Absalom!*.

Thus, for example, Irwin notes that Quentin identifies both with Henry, the brother as protector, and with Bon, the brother as seducer, but notes that this is not extraordinary as Quentin projects on to these two figures opposing elements in his own personality:

> [. . .] Bon represents Quentin's unconsciously motivated desire for his sister Candace, while Henry represents the conscious repression or punishment of that desire. (Irwin 1975, 28)

But this, I would argue, inverts the real connection. It is strictly true, as

Irwin says, that within the novel we are led to see Quentin objectifying his internal divisions through simultaneous projection on to the two half-brothers, one of whom eventually slays the other for asserting his intention to marry their sister. But the more important message of the book, it seems to me, is that the divisions in Quentin *stem from* and symbolize a society still not acknowledging and expiating the exploitation of itself by itself, of blacks by whites, in the past.

Thus it is noteworthy that Irwin talks very interestingly of Quentin's splitting of himself into two to resolve otherwise irresolvable conflicts very much in the manner of the cases of multiple personality that I looked at in my first chapter. But whereas Irwin sees these tensions primarily as archetypal Oedipal ones, when he actually quotes from *Absalom, Absalom!* to substantiate his point the focus of Faulkner's account is seen to be significantly different. Irwin argues that

> This separation of the unacceptable elements from the acceptable elements in the self, this splitting of Quentin's personality into a bad half and a good half, with the subsequent tormenting of the good half by the bad and the punishment of the bad half by the good, involves a kind of narrative bipolarity typical of both compulsion neurosis and schizophrenia. The split is the result of the self's inability to handle ambivalence, in this case, Quentin's failure to reconcile his simultaneous attraction to and repulsion by the incestuous desire for his sister. The solution is primitive and effective: one simply splits the good-bad self into two separate people. (Irwin 1975, 28)

So far Irwin's case follows and confirms the classic pattern that we have seen in our earlier case-histories, and indeed it is not hard to find even more striking parallels than are presented by any of the case-histories in my first chapter. Stanley M. Coleman, from whose article on the double I have already quoted, gives evidence that strengthens Irwin's argument: he refers to a case in which a woman who had made sexual advances to her father took him for a stranger of the same appearance, an illusion which, according to a commentator on the case 'was a final attempt to veil the incestuous urge' (Coleman 1934, 270). Coleman goes on to argue that the vast majority of such cases indicate that ambivalent sexual feelings (which would include a conflict between sexual desire and social taboo) are responsible for the formation of the illusion of doubles.

But *Absalom, Absalom!* is a work of literature, and if Quentin's 'splitting' does have the immediate origins suggested by Irwin, it also has the function of representing much larger conflicts. As I have argued, this becomes immediately apparent as soon as Faulkner's text is quoted by Irwin to establish his case:

> Indeed, at the very beginning of the novel when he first visits Miss Rosa, Quentin is presented as a divided self: '. . . he would listen to two separate

Quentins now – the Quentin Compson preparing for Harvard in the South, the deep South dead since 1865 and people with garrulous outraged baffled ghosts, listening, having to listen, to one of the ghosts which had refused to lie still even longer than most had, telling him about old ghost-times; and the Quentin Compson who was still too young to deserve yet to be a ghost, but nevertheless having to be one for all that, since he was born and bred in the deep South the same as she was – two separate Quentins now talking to one another in the long silence of notpeople, in notlanguage . . .'. (Irwin 1975, 29)

The focus in this extract, which follows immediately after the one I have previously quoted from Irwin's book, is importantly different in emphasis. Quentin's divided self is here ascribed to his membership of a particular *society* rather than to a particular – or a universal – *family*, and this leads to a rather different reading of the novel.

This is perhaps best illustrated by turning from Quentin to Sutpen. Sutpen as a child suffers from a devastating trauma very similar in its effects to similar crucial upsets suffered by the subjects of our multiple personality case-histories in their infancies. The difference is that whereas in the latter cases the trauma leads to later division in those who have experienced the shock themselves, in the case of Sutpen the later division as the repressed shock struggles to re-emerge occurs not in himself but in his children. Sutpen, sent to the mansion belonging to a local plantation owner, in ignorance goes to the front door, and is told by the black servant who recognizes him for a poor white that he must go to the back door. At this point – and here I am in agreement with Irwin's account – Sutpen makes the fatal mistake of embarking on a quest for revenge which involves not destruction of the system of privilege and power that allows such insults to take place, but the gaining of that power and privilege so that he is in a position to use them against others. And, as Irwin points out, Sutpen is doomed periodically to repeat that affront, not as receiver but as giver: he rejects his first wife and son because of their black blood, and, through Henry, he rejects his son Bon who also has black blood, and who is killed by Henry while trying (literally and metaphorically) to enter Sutpen's house.

Quentin's divisions, then, have to be seen in terms of their existence in a society in which over a period of time the divisions of race and wealth enter the *family* in one generation and the *individual* in the next. Just as, with our cases of multiple personality, the traumas of the past have to be recognized and exorcized in order to re-unite the dual or multiple selves of the individuals concerned, so too unless the South admits the repression and exploitation upon which it has been built but which it represses through the construction of false and idealized versions of the past, then it will remain divided and neurotic, obsessed by ghosts of the past. Rosa Coldfield, at the start of *Absalom, Absalom!* understands that Quentin would rather be out among friends of his own age, but she makes him

spend a whole afternoon sitting indoors and listening while she talked
about people and events you were fortunate enough to escape yourself
[. . .]. (Faulkner 1960, 10)

Quentin's 'escape', however, is as we soon become aware, more apparent
than real. He may not have met these people, but he is in part the result of
their actions, he contains within himself their histories. Moreover it seems
apparent that the distortions in Quentin's sexual desires are directly related
to the ways in which sexuality has become corruptly intermingled with
racial and other forms of oppression in the South. Henry, with whom he
identifies so closely, is presented to us by Faulkner as

a young man grown up and living in a milieu where the other sex is
separated into three sharp divisions, separated (two of them) by a chasm
which could be crossed but one time and in but one direction – ladies,
women, females – the virgins whom gentlemen someday married, the
courtesans to whom they went while on sabbaticals to the cities, the slave
girls and women upon whom that first caste rested and to whom in
certain cases it doubtless owed the very fact of its virginity [. . .].
(Faulkner 1960, 109)

Thus it is *because* Sutpen has used women, and particularly black women, in
the way that he has that incest enters his family; he feels that he cannot
acknowledge Bon as his son because of Bon's black blood, and as he cannot
make his acknowledgement he cannot prevent Bon from courting his
daughter. Symbolically, then, Quentin's incestuous desires grow out of an
earlier denial of blood relationships, a denial that lifts the incest taboo and
allows Bon's (and, symbolically, Quentin's) desire for his sister to be
admitted.

Another way of expressing what has happened is to say that Sutpen, in
denying the humanity of those black people he exploits, is instrumental in
distorting the humanity of his daughter. It is striking that the previous
quotation from *Absalom, Absalom!* is very reminiscent of the account that
Marlow gives of his upbringing in *She Stoops to Conquer*. There too a rigid
separation of women into strictly demarcated groups comprising those who
are worshipped from afar and those who are sexually exploited rebounds
back upon the male, who finds that his division of women into such different
compartments has at the same time resulted in an inner division of himself.

On another symbolic level which, although separate is nonetheless inter-
twined with the meanings I have been discussing, Quentin's incestuous
desire for his sister – a desire for a virginity which no longer exists
– parallels his desire for the South which no longer exists but the death of
which he will not concede.

Henry was the provincial, the clown almost, given to instinctive and
violent action rather than to thinking who may have been conscious that
his fierce provincial's pride in his sister's virginity was a false quantity

which must incorporate in itself an inability to endure in order to be precious, to exist, and so must depend upon its loss, absence, to have existed at all. In fact, perhaps this is the pure and perfect incest: the brother realizing that the sister's virginity must be destroyed in order to have existed at all, taking that virginity in the person of the brother-in-law, the man whom he would be if he could become, metamorphose into, the lover, the husband; by whom he would be despoiled, choose for despoiler, if he could become, metamorphose into the sister, the mistress, the bride. (Faulkner 1960, 96)

This last tripartite division of the female sex (sister, mistress, bride) is related in important ways to the tripartite division of the previous passage I quoted from the novel (virgins, courtesans, slave-girls). The one place where the parallel seems to fail is in the third category: if the sister is the virgin, and the mistress is the courtesan, how can the bride be the slave-girl? The answer to this is suggested already in that earlier quotation: the caste of 'virgins whom gentlemen someday married' rests on the slave-girls and women, and owes to them in certain cases the very fact of their virginity. It is this confusion of sexual roles and identities stemming directly from the unacknowledged sexual exploitation of black slave-girls and women that leads to the desire to commit (Bon) and to prevent (Henry) incest, desires that lead to conflict and death within the family (Henry's killing of Bon) and, finally, conflict within the individual (Quentin's desire to commit incest but his inability to do so, leading to his final suicide).

As Irwin points out; even if Bon had been as little as a sixty-fourth black he would have counted as legally black; his white (paternal) parenthood would have had no social significance, and he would have been purely his mother's son in terms of the classifications of Southern culture. With no father acknowledged by society the incest taboo cannot be invoked. Sutpen's denial of Bon's relation to him accordingly stands symbolically for the uninterest of Southern society in the white ancestry of anyone with the least trace of black blood. Thus Quentin's implicit denial of his and Caddie's shared parenthood represents a symbolic internalization of larger denials of common blood made by Southern society in general. Treating the incest theme in terms of a generalized family fails to do justice to the way in which Faulkner indicates that the tortured families with which he is concerned are fighting out tensions and contradictions that are the historical legacy their society gives to them. Racial oppression leads to the corruption of family relationships, and the corruption of family relationships in turn becomes internalized by individuals whose divisions and doublings mimic the past social divisions and doublings of the South to which they belong.

The final impression that the reader of *Absalom, Absalom!* is left with is of a whole society working out its repressions and traumas much as the patients in our early case-studies had to work out their inner conflicts to become whole again. In both cases the past demands its price: it cannot be denied but must be exposed, acknowledged, understood and paid for. To replace the true history of the South with an idealized one which conceals the exploitation and cruelty of its slave-owning foundations is to doom oneself, like Sutpen, periodically to repeat what is fled from.

It is for this reason that I cannot accept the argument of Sidney Finkelstein when he suggests that Faulkner embraces a 'mythical harmonious past' which is the 'slave-holding South before the Civil War' (Finkelstein 1968, 184). It seems to me that rather the reverse is true, that *Absalom, Absalom!* testifies to Faulkner's appreciation of the fact that unless the South and its people rejected that sort of mythical reconstruction of history they would be doomed to be enslaved by the past, condemned to periodic re-enactments of its early cruelties. As Irwin points out, Faulkner, at one of his university conferences, claimed that the novel was in part 'the story of Quentin Compson's hatred of the bad qualities in the country he loves' (Irwin 1975, 159). Quentin is thus in the classic situation that drives people mad: he is in a double-bind. He can neither reject his country, because of his love for it, nor can he express that love fully because of his recognition and hatred of its bad qualities. It is this contradictory and sterile relationship that is so aptly symbolized in his unconsummated incestuous desire for his sister.

It is certainly true that Faulkner seems to regret the loss of some of the qualities of the old South, which he sees destroyed and replaced by the more nakedly capitalistic values epitomized by the Snopes. But he never conceals his knowledge of the fatally mixed nature of the old South. When Finkelstein argues that Faulkner, like the most rabid racist, believes that even a touch of black ancestry makes a person a Negro, he misses the point made by Irwin that Faulkner is, here, merely exposing the reality of Southern life, where this was in practice the assumption that governed social behaviour. Again, when Finkelstein quotes from *Absalom, Absalom!* Faulkner's words to the effect that the ghosts of the old South are more real than the living, he assumes that this is a glorification of the past, although I believe that it is more correct to see it as an insight into the way in which the Quentins of the South are forced to be pale shadows of their forebears because they will not admit that the South they love is founded upon corruption and exploitation.

My own view of the positive vision of the novel rests on the belief that it presents us with people aware of their inadequacy and fighting against it, and that it indicates clearly what is, historically, responsible for the dehumanization of the modern 'ghosts' of the South. Nowhere is this clearer than in Judith's comments to Quentin's grandmother when she shows her the letter from Bon:

> '[. . .] Read it if you like or dont read it if you like. Because you make so
> little impression, you see. You get born and you try this and you dont
> know why only you keep on trying it and you are born at the same time
> with a lot of other people, all mixed up with them, like trying to, having

to, move your arms and legs with strings only the same strings are hitched
to all the other arms and legs and the others all trying and they dont know
why either except that the strings are all in one another's way like five or
six people all trying to make a rug on the same loom only each one wants
to weave his own pattern into the rug; and it cant matter, you know that,
or the Ones that set up the loom would have arranged things a little
better, and yet it must matter because you keep on trying or having to
keep on trying [. . .]'. (Faulkner 1960, 127)

Surely this passage expresses very clearly the fundamental destructiveness
of a conflict between collectivity and self-seeking, and of the two the former
is arguably privileged through the metaphor of the rug-weaving task, a task
that can only be achieved collectively, not through the individual self-
seeking of the separate workers. Judith's speech ends with a plea for human
contact, a desire to pass something meaningful, some explanation, from one
hand to another. As Faulkner says, elsewhere in *Absalom, Absalom!*, 'let
flesh touch with flesh, and watch the fall of all the eggshell shibboleth of
caste and color', and it is this commitment to human solidarity, to the need
for an assertion of the common humanity of all human beings, that remains
the underlying thrust of a novel populated by characters living out old sins,
divided and fragmented by their ancestors' crimes against the humanity of
others.

Although there are differences in the way in which Jean Rhys uses a very
similar plot to that of *Absalom, Absalom!* in *Wide Sargasso Sea*, one fundamental parallel needs to be insisted upon. The divisions between white and
black, which start 'out there' in the colonial encounter between two cultures,
end up 'in here', destroying Antoinette's secure sense of self, and leading
directly to her death, a death which, like Quentin's, is self-inflicted only in a
rather limited sense. There are very important differences between the two
novels of course, not the least of which is that Antoinette is a woman, and
thus on one level almost as much subject to the exercise of arbitrary power as
are the oppressed blacks. Moreover, the differences between a slave culture
such as the American Deep South, and a Colonial culture such as that of the
West Indies, are important. Both exist through the exploitation of blacks by
whites, but the existence of a mother country fuelling the colonial process, to
which the West Indian whites belong in complex and different ways, leads to
a different situation from one in which the contradictions are all in one
geographical area, and thus less easy to deny. (Faulkner no doubt chose to
have Sutpen marry his first wife, and make his fortune, in the West Indies
precisely because it was easier to suggest that his past there was unknown to
those in his own country).

What one can, inadequately, refer to as the 'setting' of *Wide Sargasso Sea*,
is clearly crucial from the start of the novel. Literally from the start, as the
first few lines of the text indicate:

They say when trouble comes close ranks, and so the white people did.

> But we were not in their ranks. The Jamaican ladies had never approved of my mother, 'because she pretty like pretty self' Christophine said. (Rhys 1968, 15)

The novel, thus, opens with trouble between racial and political groups. Ironically, however, Antoinette and her mother are excluded from the ranks of the whites and the blacks; from the former because of their 'old white' status, their sex, their poverty and, as Christophine points out, their physical attractiveness; from the latter because of their race and colour. Maybe one can suggest a similarity to the sense of exclusion that we find in Faulkner's work: exclusion from the seductive but corrupt old South with its evils of racism and privilege; exclusion from the sordid new capitalism of the entrepreneurial Snopesian North. Antoinette's situation is paradigmatic of the alienated modernist hero or heroine – alienated from an alienated society. Just like Camus's Meursault, who lives in the Arab quarter of colonial Algeria, she belongs neither to the oppressed nor to the oppressors.

Of course historically such marginal groups were, it could be argued, relatively small and hardly significant. But in the symbolic world of the novel this marginality has an important significance. It serves to indicate that in an exploitative society all involved are, in different ways, denied the possession of their full humanity. More specifically, Antoinette's marginal position in West Indian society serves to allow a fuller exploration of the marginal position of women in general.

Antoinette's early experiences, then, are those of a rejected member of a persecuting minority:

> I never looked at any strange negro. They hated us. They called us white cockroaches. Let sleeping dogs lie. (Rhys 1968, 20)

Antoinette does not even have the security of a close relationship with her mother, or with her black friend Tia, both of whom at different points in the novel reject her. This is, it needs stressing, no conventional tale of a 'deprived upbringing', no portrayal of a merely unfortunate individual who has been unlucky in her parents and her friends. Antoinette's rejection by Tia and by her mother is directly related to the racial conflict on the island; it springs out of the process of colonial exploitation of one people by another. Tia throws a stone at her after the slave uprising in which their home is burned down; her mother rejects her after the death of her son in that fire.

As we saw in the earlier thought of Antoinette's: 'Let sleeping dogs lie', she has been taught to treat all potential human contact with circumspection, to identify human beings with danger. Her childhood has given her a basic pattern for the development of intimate human relationships: initial acceptance, warmth, security, then rejection.

> (My father, visitors, horses, feeling safe in bed – all belonged to the past.) (Rhys 1968, 15)

This pattern is presented in miniature when Antoinette is taken to visit her mother after the fire, when her mother's reason has been unhinged by her experiences of violence and loss:

I put my arms round her and kissed her. She held me so tightly that I couldn't breathe and I thought, 'It's not her.' Then, 'It must be her.' She looked at the door, then at me, then at the door again. I could not say, 'He is dead,' so I shook my head. 'But I am here, I am here,' I said, and she said 'No,' quietly. Then 'No no no' very loudly and flung me from her. I fell against the partition and hurt myself. The man and the woman were holding her arms and Christophine was there. The woman said, 'Why you bring the child to make trouble, trouble, trouble? Trouble enough without that.' (Rhys 1968, 40)

The episode is important because not only does it duplicate in miniature all of Antoinette's early experiences, but it also presages her doomed relationship with Rochester.

Such early experiences are very reminiscent of the early experiences of (often maternal) rejection of the subjects of our multiple personality case-histories, and their effect is also similar. Antoinette tries to avoid contact – social and emotional – with other people, and simultaneously starts to lose hold of her own sense of self.

I took another road, past the old sugar works and the water wheel that had not turned for years. I went to parts of Coulibri that I had not seen, where there was no road, no path, no track. And if the razor grass cut my legs and arms I would think 'It's better than people.' Black ants or red ones, tall nests swarming with white ants, rain that soaked me to the skin – once I saw a snake. All better than people.

Better. Better, better than people.

Watching the red and yellow flowers in the sun thinking of nothing, it was as if a door opened and I was somewhere else, something else. Not myself any longer. (Rhys 1968, 24)

That last indication of loss of self portrays a state almost identical to that of Golyadkin's early on in *The Double* when he meets Andrey Philippovich in inopportune circumstances and says to himself, 'It's quite all right; this is not me at all, Andrey Philippovich, it's not me at all, not me, and that's all about it' (Dostoyevsky 1972, 132). In both cases an intolerable social situation which can, nevertheless, not be denied or escaped from, leads the individual concerned to seek relief by denying him or herself instead. Just as Golyadkin starts to behave like an animal rather than a human being, hiding in a mousehole and referring to himself as an insect, so Antoinette seeks escape from human beings in the company of flowers, razor grass and ants.

The passage quoted above from *Wide Sargasso Sea* is moving in its directness, and links Antoinette's retreating sense of self with her concern for the unreliability of human contacts. We can well understand how it is that after such a traumatic upbringing a friendly gesture from another person can seem almost more threatening than aggression: friendship invites the lowering of defences, the risk of hurt, the vulnerability of committing onself to a relationship – when all previous experience has suggested that involvement in such an intimate relationship, along with all the emotional risks that this introduces, can lead only to misery and betrayal.

Many of Sylvia Plath's poems testify to a fear of gifts, and it may be that gifts, like an offer of friendship, imply a need for reciprocation. We can well understand that the person whose primary experiences have been like Antoinette's knows that it is not just the Greeks who have to be suspected when they come bearing gifts. As R.D. Laing suggests in *The Divided Self*, to the schizophrenic hating and being hated may be felt to threaten loss of identity less than do loving and being loved. One of the cruel aspects of Rochester's courtship of Antoinette is that he persuades her to lift her defences, to engage in a risk-taking human relationship one more time.

Talking to Rochester, after her marriage, Antoinette relates her feeling of lost identity specifically to the larger contradictions of the colonial situation:

> 'Did you hear what the girl was singing?' Antoinette said.
> 'I don't always understand what they say or sing.' Or anything else.
> 'It was a song about a white cockroach. That's me. That's what they call all of us who were here before their own people in Africa sold them to the slave traders. And I've heard English women call us white niggers. So between you I often wonder who I am and where is my country and where do I belong and why was I ever born at all. Will you go now please. I must dress like Christophine said.' (Rhys 1968, 85)

As I have suggested already, I think that it would be a mistake to assume that Jean Rhys's examination of Antoinette's alienation is merely a concern with a special, 'tragic', case. It is not that in an otherwise reasonable system in which people belong either to one group or another a few individuals get stuck on the edges and belong to neither. Antoinette's collapse is not an exception to more typical experiences in her society, it is representative of them. *Wide Sargasso Sea* as much as *Absalom, Absalom!* reveals that a society in which one group consistently and shamelessly exploits another will divide the members of the exploiting group as much as it divides itself between the two groups. Antoinette's collapse is no more external to the dominant processes of her society than Quentin Compson's is to his; her betrayal and fragmentation are the result of a system that betrays and fragments its members' own humanity. It is no accident that Antoinette's final, ultimately destructive betrayal is by a man from the 'mother' country, completing the process of maternal rejection that is to drive her mad. Rochester's behaviour is intimately related to a colonial system which breeds self-interest and individualism, and supresses emotion in favour of 'duty'.

Thus we learn that Rochester's upbringing has already schooled him to play a part when he comes to the island; his whole education has been a process of learning to suppress his natural emotions, a suppression that it is most necessary that a colonial administrator should learn.

> How old was I when I learned to hide what I felt? A very small boy. Six, five, even earlier. It was necessary, I was told, and that view I have always accepted. If these mountains challenge me, or Baptiste's face, or Antoinette's eyes, they are mistaken, melodramatic, unreal (England must be quite unreal and like a dream she said). (Rhys 1968, 85)

Mrs G told Robert Stoller that her dissociated personality Charlie did not want her to start feeling, in order to protect her: her repression of feelings had started as a child when she was scared all the time. But the above passage shows very clearly that for Rochester here it is the requirements of the colonial situation that have led to his having been schooled so to suppress his feelings and emotions – and above all else to hide them.

Suppression of the emotions can – to state an obvious point – lead to repression and trauma. Such suppression involves acting a part, becoming a person who is foreign to your actual sense of your self. In his account of 'Ruth' in his book *The Story of Ruth*, Morton Schatzman gives an interesting account of her attendance at her grandmother's funeral. We know from other accounts that a mother's or grandmother's funeral can be an extremely traumatic experience in the lives of those who later experience dissociation; Sybil's first dissociative experience seems to have been at the graveside while her grandmother was being interred. This is Ruth's own description in a letter to Schatzman:

> I couldn't believe she was dead. She looked so real, only younger. She had on a blue satin gown with long sleeves and a high collar laced around the neck. She looked beautiful. She was cold, and her flesh felt hard. I couldn't stand up any longer. I sat in a chair near her. They were going to bury her in two hours. I stayed by her until they moved her to the chapel. I felt closer to her than I had in my whole life. Everyone kept telling my mama that I needed her, but I didn't. I wanted to cry and mourn all alone. At the chapel service I couldn't stand it. The preacher meant well but he kept saying things he knew nothing about. They played her favorite hymns, which she used to sing to me when she rocked me. I didn't break down, because Grandma had said never to show your feelings for outsiders to see. (Schatzman 1980, 173)

In an autobiographical fragment entitled 'A Sketch of the Past,' Virginia Woolf describes a set of experiences arising out of the death of her own mother which are strikingly similar to those described by Ruth.

> I remember very clearly how even as I was taken to the bedside I noticed that one nurse was sobbing, and a desire to laugh came over me, and I said to myself as I have often done at moments of crisis since, 'I feel nothing whatever'. Then I stooped and kissed my mother's face. It was still warm. [. . .]

> Perhaps it was the next evening that Stella took me into the bedroom to kiss mother for the last time. [. . .] When I kissed her, it was like kissing cold iron. (Woolf 1981, 107)

In the same account Virginia Woolf talks of her hallucinated vision of a man sitting on the bed with her dead mother. Moreover, according to Nancy Topping Bazin, Virginia Woolf wrote that 'the chrysalis of her childhood split in two', when at the age of fifteen she felt the full impact of her mother's death (Bazin 1973, 40). The relationship between the juvenile experience of intolerable emotional hurt, a developed propensity to feel nothing at times of subsequent anguish, and the experience of personality bifurcation could hardly be indicated more clearly than in the accounts of Ruth and of Virginia Woolf.

Jean Rhys's Rochester also relates an early schooling in the suppression of emotion with his later, almost dissociated behaviour. But there is a difference. His suppression of emotions has a function sanctioned by his society. He has been taught to ignore the demands of the humanity of the colonized ('If these mountains challenge me, or Baptiste's face, or Antoinette's eyes; they are mistaken'), so that he can successfully maintain the illusions of colonialism that are essential to the running of the system. But as we have seen, 'Antoinette's eyes' have to be denied along with 'Baptiste's face'; to reject the reality of the black experience of colonialism is also to reject part of the whites' knowledge of it, and this is what leads to alienation from one's self.

The point is repeated when Rochester meets Antoinette, where it is apparent that in order to behave 'in the right way', Rochester has to deny aspects of his own humanity, and watch himself acting a part:

> It was all very brightly coloured, very strange, but it meant nothing to me. Nor did she, the girl I was to marry. When at last I met her I bowed, smiled, kissed her hand, danced with her. I played the part I was expected to play. She never had anything to do with me at all. Every movement I made was an effort of will and sometimes I wondered that no one noticed this. I would listen to my own voice and marvel at it, calm, correct but toneless, surely. But I must have given a faultless performance. If I saw an expression of doubt or curiosity it was on a black face not a white one. (Rhys 1968, 64)

That this play acting is related to the larger social and cultural pressures within which Rochester and Antoinette have been raised is, surely, made clear. Rochester's is the stiff upper lip of the English colonialist, suppressing his own humanity in order to be able to suppress the humanity of others.

The very style in which Rochester's thoughts are expressed mimics a practised inner monologue of the sort used to conceal one's feelings from outsiders. The dulled, guilt-free cynicism of the expression indicates how effective Rochester's education has been in teaching him to witness pain feeling it. He is portrayed as one who measures human relationships in cash rather than in human terms, regretting that, 'I have not bought her, she has bought me, or so she thinks' (Rhys 1968, 59). Having suppressed his feelings for aspects of himself for so long he finds it relatively easy to suppress them for Antoinette and the demands of her humanity.

> 'You are safe,' I'd say. She'd liked that – to be told 'you are safe.' Or I'd touch her face gently and touch tears. Tears – nothing! Words – less than nothing. I did not love her. I was thirsty for her, but that is not love. I felt very little tenderness for her, she was a stranger to me, a stranger who did not think or feel as I did. (Rhys 1968, 78)

Antoinette is described by Rochester here in the manner in which oppressed people have traditionally been described by their oppressors; his words call to mind the much-publicized comments made by an American general about the Vietnamese people. Such peoples, oppressors have been fond of assuring themselves and others, are not 'like us', they are 'simple' or 'savage', strangers who think and feel differently from the way 'we' do. Antoinette's betrayal is involved in – is an extension of – the betrayal of their own humanity that the whites have committed by oppressing the blacks. Rochester uses weapons on Antoinette that have been developed for black people.

And just as the white colonialist turns the black person into someone or something foreign to his or her real identity, so Rochester starts to transform Antoinette into another person. Just as Sybil's parents confuse her sense of self by giving her different names, so Rochester starts to call Antoinette by a different name from the name she accepts as her own. Again, it is a common technique of the imperialist and colonialist to impose an alien language with alien terms on to the people who are to be exploited, so that they start to see themselves as their oppressors see them. It is for this reason that the rejection of 'slave names' has such a significant symbolic import.

Antoinette's experience with names is oddly like the real experiences of Mrs G and of Sybil. Mrs G

> was given her father's first name. It is an unusual name, and with different spelling is either male or female. Whether it was due to coincidence or the unconscious plans parents have for their infants, no more apt name could have been chosen to reflect bisexuality. However, Mrs G's parents could not leave it at that: they added more names. From earliest childhood (perhaps from birth on), although she officially bore her father's name, she was called by an endearing, more feminine nickname, 'Sugar'. Then, when she started kindergarten, the teachers chose to call her by her middle name, an unquestionably feminine name, but to the child an alien sound to which she did not respond with the feeling that it was she who had been addressed.
>
> All of this is to say that without a name one lacks an essential part of oneself. (Stoller 1974, 195)

In Sybil's case her father chose her name, but her mother did not like it and proceeded to confuse her sense of self by giving her another. The child's sense of being forced to be different people for her two parents was thus objectified in two different names, and it is not surprising that one of her later personalities took the name of her mother's choice. Antoinette finds the same denial of her essential identity in Rochester's treatment of her:

> 'Bertha is not my name. You are trying to make me into someone else, calling me by another name. I know, that's obeah [*witchcraft, JH*] too.' (Rhys 1968, 121)

Antoinette's account of her mother's descent into madness makes it quite clear that this was the result not of any internal or organic weakness, but of her situation of poverty, loneliness and isolation. Her own position parallels that of her mother's; repeated betrayals have left Antoinette so isolated, so unsure of who she is, that Rochester's treatment of her constitutes the last straw.

It is worth noting that to the end the racial division on the island permeates the relationship. Rochester's mind is poisoned by the 'cousin's' slander, a slander that comes from a man himself embittered by racial prejudices and corruptions. It is a black servant girl with whom Rochester sleeps, in the room next to Antoinette's. And the potential relationship of trust and equality between Antoinette and Sandi never develops, rendered impossible by his colour. When Sandi helps her, towards the start of the novel, racist divisions come between the two of them irrespective of their personal integrity:

> 'You dropped this,' he said, and smiled. I knew who he was, his name was Sandi, Alexander Cosway's son. Once I would have said 'my cousin Sandi' but Mr Mason's lectures had made me shy about my coloured relatives. I muttered, 'Thank you.' (Rhys 1968, 42)

It is not accidental, surely, that the boy from whose aggression Sandi protects her is a half-caste; as with Faulkner the half-caste symbolizes the human internalization of external divisions in a racially divided society. Antoinette is oppressed by the results of her forefather's racial oppression of others. As we learn at the end of the novel, when Sandi calls upon her to go with him, she cannot; barriers of wealth, race and power prevent her.

And barriers of another sort. Antoinette is a woman. Rochester may be just as divided and as lonely as she, but he has wealth, he has power, and thus he has more control over his life than she has. As Grace Poole thinks, back in England with Antoinette,

> *After all the house is big and safe, a shelter from the world outside which, say what you like, can be a black and cruel world to a woman.* (Rhys 1968, 146)

It seems hardly accidental that a woman's world is *black*; the subordination to the power of men suffered by women is, for Antoinette, a duplication of the oppression of black by white. Small wonder that when she finally asserts herself it is by means of the weapon used by the rebelling blacks earlier in her life in the West Indies: by means of fire. Like the final conflagration in *Absalom, Absalom!* this has the effect of asserting the need for social and political liberation in order to achieve personal, existential liberation.

Both of these two novels, then, indicate that the divisions that oppression, racism and exploitation introduce into a society are not purely external things. They enter into the souls of oppressors and oppressed in innumerable, complex ways. But whereas the oppressed can find a common humanity in their shared persecution, a humanity that can be asserted in the struggle against oppression, the oppressors are cut off even from one another as a result of their behaviour. And it is only by joining in the fight of the oppressed that they can regain their own humanity. That both novels end with white people using the fire, the weapon of the oppressed, suggests that Faulkner and Jean Rhys were well aware of this fact at the level of their creative imaginations.

8

Sales and Solidarity: Arthur Miller's *Death of a Salesman*

The very title, *Death of a Salesman*, directs our attention to the relationship between the personal and the commercial, the individual and the employee. In 1948, when the play was first performed and the Cold War had well and truly started, Miller's work evoked the same sort of interest as had been aroused by *She Stoops to Conquer* nearly two centuries previously, and for not dissimilar reasons. Both plays concern themselves directly with issues so central to their respective societies that their audiences responded to them as to personal revelations. As we saw earlier with Lucy Snowe, in her surprise to discover Polly's thoughts so similar to her own, a society which privatizes and represses certain feelings does not allow its members to discover that their secret fantasies and their apparently idiosyncratic impulses are common to many. One of the most positive aspects of art and literature is that they work against such concealments, allowing the individual to discover himself or herself in other people – and vice-versa. It is because Arthur Miller confronts problems central to his time and his society in *Death of a Salesman* that he is able to touch the private and personal concerns of his characters – and his audience – so effectively.

Part of Miller's genius perhaps consisted in his having chosen a *salesman* as hero. The very name of the profession triggers off just the right contradictory responses: representative on the one hand of the capitalist ethic, commerce, free enterprise, individual initiative and personal achievement (along with the geographical and social mobility so much a part of the American Dream), but on the other hand with a reputation for double-dealing, hypocrisy, easy morality and the ethics of the rat-race. When American voters were asked whether or not they would buy a used car from Nixon, they were being encouraged to recognize precisely the same sort of untrustworthiness in the politician as they knew had to be guarded against in the salesman.

Willy Loman's fragmentation, then, has to be seen as an exaggerated version of what people already associated with salesmen; people whose private thoughts were at variance with their public professions. As with all such forms of knowledge, however, this awareness of the gap between the commercial and the human is a partial one for most people in a capitalist society; it is there to be used in practical situations, it will be admitted when people are explicitly asked about it, but its implications are rarely followed through. The reasons for this can be found within Miller's play: there is a continuous barrage of propaganda to deny that this is the case, sometimes direct propaganda, but more often than not indirect and subtle.

Let me, prior to looking in detail at *Death of A Salesman*, give an example of what I mean. Barbara O'Brien's book *Operators and Things* is an account of a schizophrenic breakdown suffered by the writer, a breakdown which took the form of her experiencing severe hallucinations, in which various odd and threatening individuals gave her orders and advice which she, believing in their real existence, followed. O'Brien starts her account with a description of the pressures she felt subject to at work, a description which calls to mind Golyadkin's and Aikeky Aikeyevitch's office nightmares, and which suggests that some forms of social pressure are crystallized in tensions at work. O'Brien picks out one business technique which she names 'hook operating.'

> I've made some sharp revisions in my ideas of how people get ahead fast in business since the day I looked at Ken [*a colleague*] and saw how clear it all was. The thing you need is a special kind of skill that Ken didn't have and could never have developed. It's the technique of the Hook Operator. (O'Brien 1976, 30)

According to O'Brien, success in business follows implementation of the techniques of hook operating. The hook operator, once he (and it normally is he, not she) enters a business organization, noses out the person with power. He then finds his weak spot and wounds it either to discredit another person (the rival), or to make himself essential to the 'Powerman'.

Such a summary does scant justice to O'Brien's lengthy account of the techniques of getting ahead in business, but it does indicate its main points. In the organization in which she worked there were two such operators: Gordon and McDermott. Of them she comments:

> [. . .] there are too many men like Gordon and McDermott for me to feel now that all of them are twisted. In a way, they have adapted themselves superbly to a certain type of business environment. Both Gordon and McDermott cut the most direct road they could find to where they wanted to go. That they both knifed a few men getting there was totally unimportant to either of them. [. . .] Christian principles are not the principles on which the Hook Operators build their lives, although this fact, so glaringly obvious to others, is rarely apparent to the Hook Operators. I think that the strangest thing I knew about either Gordon or McDermott was that both were extremely religious men. (O'Brien 1976, 35)

There are two crucial insights in this passage, to which I wish to draw attention. Firstly, that the *primary* contradiction is not in the people themselves but in the type of business environment to which they have adapted, and secondly that this adaptation has turned them into divided and contradictory people, although they don't know this and feel themselves to be perfectly normal and consistent.

O'Brien's breakdown is a classic example of how the person who tries to remain consistent, in an environment which demands inconsistency, is driven mad. Her breakdown took the form not of a personality split in the manner of my earlier case-histories, but of hallucinations in which, among other things, personified hook operators appeared and explained the world to her. However, what I find most interesting of all in her account, and most directly relevant to Willy Loman's case, is that in spite of the fact that she is amazed to discover that neither McDermott nor Gordon recognize the contradictions in the values according to which they live, she too ends up by blaming her breakdown, in a curiously confused passage, not on her situation but upon herself:

> I seem to be blaming my community for a personal tragedy. I am not. There was nothing particularly wrong with it and there was a great deal in it that was right. It was a civilized community. The tragedy was that, overnight, certain jungle qualities appeared faster than I could adjust to them. The error lay, not in the community in which I was reared but in the way in which I, as an individual, adapted to it. I departmentalized, burying elements inside of me which should never have been buried and as a consequence lost wholeness to gain acceptance for a part of me. (O'Brien 1976, 140)

As I say, this seems to me to be confused, indeed, almost neurotic in its refusal to place the blame where all her earlier arguments lead – in the ethics of the business community. To call the community civilized is directly at variance with what she has earlier described as the perfect fit between the techniques of the hook operators and the business community to which they are adapted. It is odd that, in the passage just quoted, the civilized community is distinguished from 'certain jungle qualities' which just 'appeared' – the vague grammatical formulation serving to obscure whether or not the jungle qualities are part of the so-called civilized community or, as is here hinted if not explicitly stated, somehow extraneous to them.

I find this process of equivocation and contradiction very significant indeed. Let me explain why by drawing a parallel with Miss Beauchamp's case. We can hypothesize that a key contradiction in her case – if not the key contradiction – lay in the ambivalent attitude towards sexuality of her society. If you were respectable, then you were not sexually excited by improper conversation and behaviour. Finding that she was sexually excited by these, Miss Beauchamp had, we may hypothesize, two alternatives. Either she could decide that the accepted views of her society were wrong: nice girls *were* also subject to sexual excitement as a result of behaviour not considered proper, or she could decide that society was right and that therefore she was not a nice girl. We can further hypothesize that Miss Beauchamp felt incapable of condemning society and its double standards vis-a-vis sexual morality and behaviour, and so she was forced to conclude that the fault lay in her. However, being unable to accept either that she had not been sexually aroused by Mr Jones, or that she was not respectable, she resolved the irresolveable by becoming two people: one respectable person and one person subject to improper sexual excitement. (I should make it clear that although I find this a defensible interpretation of part of Miss Beauchamp's personality fragmentation, it is clearly not the whole story.)

In Barbara O'Brien's case we can see that, by refusing to locate that double-standard she deplores in society, by failing to see that her society claims to be a Christian society but also runs its businesses according to the law of the jungle, she forces herself to ascribe her breakdown to her own inadequacy. The pattern is directly applicable to Willy Loman's case. He is neither unimaginative enough to act as did McDermott and Gordon and proceed oblivious of the fact that there are contradictions in his life (although it is perhaps the case that he tries to do this but fails), nor can he recognize the larger double standards central and essential to his job and the capitalist social system. He believes the version of the American Dream that comes from the Chevrolet advertisements in the glossy magazines, and he tries to fit his actual life experiences into this mythic pattern. When the two won't fit he refuses to acknowledge the fact until he is first of all split into two people and, finally, destroyed. (Although he commits suicide it is also legitimate to see his death as something that is imposed upon him by outside forces.) Like Barbara O'Brien, Willy Loman refuses to blame his job or his society for inculcating false and contradictory values, perhaps because these values have become so much a part of his view of himself that to attack them would involve reconstructing enormous aspects of himself. We can see a similar pattern in Virginia Woolf's *Mrs Dalloway*, in which novel Septimus, the 'mad' character, at one point muses that as his brain is perfect, 'It must be the fault of the world then – that he could not feel.' But the medical profession takes it upon itself to prove that it is in fact Septimus, not the world, that is at fault, and he too commits suicide. We can perhaps venture a generalization here: if a person is subjected to intolerable and contradictory pressures from society, family or work, but insists upon seeing these pressures as normal, uncontradictory and manageable, then he or she will be forced to conclude that the fault is in him or herself.

This leads us to the vexed issue of ideology, around which there has been much debate in recent years, and to which I have at this moment scant desire to add much comment. *Death of a Salesman* is a play which forces us to consider the issue of ideology however, as Willy Loman's breakdown is so clearly associated with the ideological pressures placed upon him by his work and his society. One of Willy's problems is that like Septimus he refuses to compartmentalize; he tries to behave to others and to himself in a consistent way. Paradoxically, of course, this has the effect of splitting him in two. During my discussion of Dostoyevsky's *The Double* in an earlier chapter I quoted from Ludwig *et al.* (1972) to the effect that the separate functioning of different personalities may represent a more effective way of handling anxiety than a coalescence of identities in one, integrated personality. I commented then that it may not just be a better way of handling anxiety, but a better way of handling contradictions in society. The point is germane to a discussion of Willy Loman's case. Willy's problem is not that he is divided, but that he cannot keep his separate identities apart. It is not that he is affected by the Chevrolet advertisement or by dreams of his son becoming a great football player – that much must have been true of millions of Americans – but that when his actual experiences fail to measure up to these ideologically imposed myths he attempts to paper over reality with the myth. Another way of putting it is to suggest that Willy's problem is not that he is divided, but that he is not divided enough: we can recall that Wemmick's life starts to become problematic for him only when his 'country' personality intrudes into his 'town' existence. Willy's mistake is, as Charley points out at the end of the play, that he allows the dreams necessary to his work to start to take over his whole person.

> Nobody dast blame this man. You don't understand; Willy was a salesman. And for a salesman, there is no rock bottom to the life. He don't put a bolt to a nut, he don't tell you the law or give you medicine. He's a man way out there in the blue, riding on a smile and a shoeshine. And when they start not smiling back – that's an earthquake. And then you get yourself a couple of spots on your hat, and you're finished. Nobody dast blame this man. A salesman is got to dream, boy. It comes with the territory. (Miller 1968, 111)

If it is significant that Herbert Pocket and Pip make their fortune abroad, it is equally revealing that Willy Loman's dream is associated with the myth of the frontiersman, the man who solves all the contradictions of his social relationships by geographical movement, by lighting out to a new territory, in which things can all start afresh. But Willy's 'territory' is not virgin land: it is the capitalist jungle, and its problems cannot be solved through individual effort.

As Charley points out, the salesman is, as it were, almost the personification of pure exchange: he does not engage in productive labour, he doesn't help people directly, he sells, and he also sells himself. Thus when people stop smiling back it means not only that you are failing at your job, but also that you are forced to see the other side of that freedom from human contact that in one part of the myth you prize. As Charley says, you have got to dream, 'It comes with the territory', you have to lead a fantasy life because your workaday life is denuded of all real human contact. It is important to recognize, therefore, that Willy's dreams are not just personal idiosyncrasies, but necessary products of his job as a salesman. We can suggest, though, that whereas the dream usually functions as a *compensation* for the life the salesman has to lead, Willy tries to impose it on that life, to see his whole existence in terms of this compensatory dream. And, paradoxically, by trying to lead a consistent, undivided life, he ends up separating it into dream and reality.

Biff comes to see this. He says that Willy had the wrong dreams, and he looks at the pen he has just stolen, a theft which at this point in the play seems to epitomize a particular set of qualities: individualism, self-seeking and hardness. He asks himself

> what the hell am I grabbing this for? Why am I trying to become what I don't want to be? What am I doing in an office, making a contemptuous, begging fool of myself, when all I want is out there, waiting for me the minute I say I know who I am? (Miller 1968, 105)

The insight here is, I feel, only partial, and its incompleteness is perhaps as much Miller's as it is Biff's. Biff still believes that the escape from such contradictions is an individual thing, dependent upon 'knowing who you are', even if he does recognize that there are pressures on people to be what is unnatural to them. The idea that one might have a very good perception of who one is, but still be unable to allow this perceived identity full play in a society that is not run on exclusively human lines is missing. There is thus a case for arguing that although *Death of a Salesman* attacks the American Dream through Willy, there is a certain amount of ideological recuperation through Biff. If all we had to do was recognize who we were, and act upon it, then clearly Willy is personally responsible for his collapse.

In many ways the play is split between a recognition of the falsity of the dream of individual salvation, with the implication that the society that fosters such dreams is at fault, and a view that is itself fundamentally individualistic, that human beings have to work out their own salvation and choose the right life for themselves. Thus in the early conversation between Biff and Happy about going out West, the unreal nature of this solution to their problems is clearly signposted:

> *Biff:* [*with enthusiasm*]: Listen, why don't you come out West with me?
> *Happy:* You and I, heh?
> *Biff:* Sure, maybe we could buy a ranch. Raise cattle, use our muscles. Men built like we are should be working in the open.
> *Happy:* [*avidly*]: The Loman Brothers, heh? (Miller 1968, 17)

This solution, clearly shown as an impossible dream at this stage of the play, is the one actually chosen in a modified form by Biff at the end of the play.

Willy is a man who has never realized that his dreams are dreams, and may offer him some comfort for the life he has to lead, but can never actually be lived. In one sense this is what marks out his moral stature: he refuses to accept the existence – or the power – of the sordid commercial values that dominate his working life. When he gets no help from Howard, the son of his old boss who he actually named, he is surprised; he believes that his human relationship with Howard and his father mean that he can expect human treatment by them. Charley tells him the truth:

Willy, when're you gonna realize that them things don't mean anything? You named him Howard, but you can't sell that. The only thing you got in this world is what you can sell. And the funny thing is that you're a salesman, and you don't know that. (Miller 1968, 76)

Such blindness, we are led to feel, is to a certain extent one of Willy's endearing qualities; to fail in a society in which the price of success is so high may indicate a humanity that is not to be despised. And Willy's belief that human values really count that much in the commercial world is, after all, a belief that is fostered in his (and our) society. As the authors of *Love and Commitment* put it:

The profusion of images of love in our culture makes it appear as if they can penetrate any social context. They never depict exchange occurring in solidarity contexts. Moreover, there is no social context which these images cannot encompass. For example, we are shown interracial couples drinking in harmony in neighborhood bars in working-class communities. More insidiously, these images portray solidarity and exchange as perfectly compatible [. . .]. (Schwarz and Merten 1980, 254)

They go on to suggest, in a comment to which I have already made reference, that whereas in contemporary American culture solidarity is vulnerable to transformation by exchange principles, people are led to believe that it is the reverse that is actually the case. This is what Willy believes: that his human relationships with others are more important (which they are) and more powerful (which, immediately, they are not) than the arguments of cash and commerce.

In my earlier discussion of Barbara O'Brien's book, I quoted a comment of hers in which she referred to 'jungle qualities' which appeared in her business community. The word 'jungle' appears a number of times in *Death of a Salesman* and represents precisely those same qualities of unprincipled self-seeking and ambition described by Barbara O'Brien. The character who personifies them in the play is Ben who, in a mock fight with the young Biff, trips him up and threatens his eye with an umbrella:

Ben: [*patting* Biff's *knee*]: Never fight fair with a stranger, boy. You'll never get out of the jungle that way. (Miller 1968, 38)

If Willy imposes his human dream on the inhuman world, Ben imposes the values of his inhuman world on his human relationships.

Willy's problem, though, is that the inhuman world keeps tripping him up, holding an umbrella to his eye, and demanding that he recognize its existence. Thus Willy gets agitated and angry when he senses that reality is going to break into his dream:

Linda: When you write you're coming, he's all smiles, and talks about the future, and − he's just wonderful. And then the closer you seem to come, the more shaky he gets, and then, by the time you get here, he's arguing, and he seems angry at you. (Miller 1968, 42)

The reality of Biff and Happy cannot mesh in with the fantasy picture of them that Willy has, a picture which clearly Willy has not constructed from nothing, but which he has absorbed from the myths of his culture. When I hear the following imaginary speech of Willy's to his young sons, it reminds me of nothing more than those car advertisements in glossy American magazines of the 1940s and 1950s:

Willy: I been wondering why you polish the car so careful. Ha! Don't leave the hubcaps, boys. Get the chamois to the hubcaps. Happy, use newspaper on the windows, it's the easiest thing. Show him how to do it, Biff! You see, Happy? Pad it up, use it like a pad. That's it, that's it, good work. You're doin' all right, Hap. [*He pauses, then nods in approbation for a few seconds, then looks upward.*] Biff, first thing we gotta do when we get time is clip that big branch over the house. Afraid it's gonna fall in a storm and hit the roof. [. . .] (Miller 1968, 21)

The gap between the world of advertisements and reality is more or less explicitly referred to when Willy contradicts himself so starkly about his refrigerator and his car. Willy tells Linda that the 'Chevrolet [. . .] is the greatest car ever built', then a few moments later, learning that he still owes money on the carburettor (something they don't normally talk about in car advertisements), he explodes, 'That goddam Chevrolet, they ought to prohibit the manufacture of that car!'

What Willy says of the refrigerator is true of himself:

Once in my life I would like to own something outright before it's broken! I'm always in a race with the junkyard! I just finished paying for the car and it's on its last legs. The refrigerator consumes belts like a goddam maniac. They time those things. They time them so when you finally paid for them, they're used up. (Miller 1968, 56)

On the day that Linda makes the last payment on the house, she also buries Willy. He too has been a victim of planned obsolescence; when he has no more cash value, his humanity is discarded. As Willy says to Howard, he has been used like an orange; the fruit has been eaten and the peel – Willy himself – is thrown away.

Willy Loman's fragmentation, then, cannot be seen simply as the result of a fatal flaw in him, an inability to work out who he is or what he wants. He swallows the tales he is told, but he cannot digest them. Only by blackmailing people to share his fantasies can he maintain them for a limited period, but eventually, like all those who try to live in a divided society as if it were undivided, he is crushed. Ben survives, because the laws of the jungle can be imposed upon the human world in his society, whereas Willy discovers that in America the laws of the truly human cannot be imposed upon the jungle. As Schwarz and Merten put it, solidarity cannot penetrate exchange relationships; love does not conquer all.

In Brecht's *The Good Person of Setzuan* the heroine, Shen Te, learns the lesson indicated by Ludwig *et al.*; the separate functioning of alter identities can in certain circumstances be a more effective way of surviving than the creation of a consistent and integrated personality. In her and Willy Loman's divisions we see comparable insights into the nature of societies which, paradoxically, insist that their members divide themselves in order to stay whole. But in the last resort, whereas Brecht moves from this insight to a clear indication that society must needs be changed, Miller's conclusion retreats from the implications of his earlier analysis.

9
The Bell Jar and the Larger Things: Sylvia Plath

> I saw my life branching out before me like the green fig-tree in the story.
>
> From the tip of every branch, like a fat purple fig, a wonderful future beckoned and winked. One fig was a husband and a happy home and children, and another fig was a famous poet and another fig was a brilliant professor, and another fig was Ee Gee, the amazing editor, and another fig was Europe and Africa and South America, and another fig was Constantin and Socrates and Attila and a pack of other lovers with queer names and off-beat professions, and another fig was an Olympic lady crew champion, and beyond and above these figs were many more figs I couldn't quite make out.
>
> I saw myself sitting in the crotch of this fig-tree, starving to death, just because I couldn't make up my mind which of the figs I would choose. I wanted each and every one of them, but choosing one meant losing all the rest, and, as I sat there, unable to decide, the figs began to wrinkle and go black, and, one by one, they plopped to the ground at my feet. (Plath 1966, 80)

For Esther Greenwood, heroine of Sylvia Plath's *The Bell Jar*, the choice between mutually exclusive futures clearly poses problems which are related to her later breakdown. Moreover, this choice between these mutually exclusive alternatives is related not just to what she does, but to what she is; the novel indicates from its opening pages that Esther's confusion and despair stem from her having to act a part in various social activities which are little more than charades for her, charades with little or no relationship to her actual feelings and inclinations. It is only in her fantasies that these real feelings and inclinations can be indulged.

Esther, at the start of the novel, is thus in a state comparable to that of Golyadkin at the start of Dostoyevsky's *The Double*: playing a part in society which necessitates the repression and concealment of real feelings, emotions, and desires. It is interesting, therefore, to remember that Sylvia Plath completed an undergraduate dissertation on the theme of the double in two of Dostoyevsky's novels: *The Double* and *The Brothers Karamazov*. There is evidence in this dissertation, written in 1955 (five or so years before the writing of *The Bell Jar*) that Plath used the exercise of writing the study to explore aspects of her own breakdown which had occurred shortly before the writing of the dissertation, and which clearly provides much of the material which is used to create *The Bell Jar*. Plath compares Golyadkin's 'personality structure' to that of a victim of acute schizophrenia, drawing upon information in an article on schizophrenia by Edward W. Lazell included in a contemporary textbook *Modern Abnormal Psychology*, edited by William H. Mikesell (1950). Plath quotes Lazell to the effect that schizophrenia represents a definite type of personality disorganization which limits the patient's ability to adapt himself to reality. The patient's early experiences and conflicts are seen to have caused the repression of instinctive urges and cravings, producing – inevitably – feelings of guilt and insecurity.

Plath accepts this as an adequate explanation of Golyadkin's dissociation, commenting however, that as we meet him 'on the very morning of his schizophrenic outbreak, we cannot be sure of the exact nature of his "early experiences and conflicts" ' (Plath 1955, 10). Plath's analysis is an interesting one and, bearing in mind the far more limited general knowledge concerning schizophrenia at the time she was writing, a strikingly original one for a young undergraduate. But what is very apparent when we compare this account of breakdown with that given in *The Bell Jar* is that the roots of Esther Greenwood's collapse are not seen to be exclusively situated in her individual past, but are present at large in the world in which she is living. 'Roots' may indeed be an inappropriate metaphor: it is Esther's perception of the constraints her society places upon her in terms of her present and her future that is intimately related to her breakdown. From the undergraduate dissertation to the novel, then, there is a significant shift of emphasis from the individual's personal history of childhood repression to the pressure exerted upon a mature individual by his or her society. This is not to say that Plath discounts the importance of such early experiences: both in *The Bell Jar* and autobiographical fragments (including references in, and to, poems) Plath stresses the traumatic effect of the death of a father for a young child, and the double-binding nature of other familial relationships. But these experiences are seen in dialectical relation with other, more 'normal' social pressures in the later investigations into breakdown. It is perhaps worth recalling that our earlier consideration of multiple-personality case-histories indicated that both childhood trauma and repression, and adult crisis were needed to precipitate personality dissociation.

What *The Bell Jar* makes particularly clear is that the problems Esther faces in her young adult life are peculiar, for the most part, to the experience of a *woman*. For a man, getting married and being a famous editor – or having children and becoming a famous poet – are not mutually exclusive options. Esther's 'fig-tree' dilemma is not just one which faces anyone trying to decide between different careers; it is specifically the problem of a woman not granted the luxury of a *double* life. Esther is sent an article by her mother on female chastity, cut out from the *Reader's Digest*. This clipping forefronts the whole issue of male double standards for Esther, especially as she has just learned that the seemingly (and avowedly) pure Buddy Willard has had an affair with a waitress:

> Now the one thing this article didn't seem to me to consider was how a girl felt.
>
> It might be nice to be pure and then to marry a pure man, but what if he suddenly confessed he wasn't pure after we were married, the way Buddy Willard had? I couldn't stand the idea of a woman having to have a single pure life and a man being able to have a double life, one pure and one not. (Plath 1966, 85)

Things have not changed so much since the time Goldsmith wrote *She Stoops to Conquer*; women are still expected to be either one thing or another while men have the freedom to be both.

In *The Bell Jar* the younger women are, in general, either virgins or whores, wives or mistresses – compartmentalized in a way roughly comparable to the female divisions outlined by Faulkner in *Absalom, Absalom!*, but without the complication of racial divisions as well. For a sensitive and thinking woman such as Esther the choices are unsatisfactory: the 'whores' like Doreen or the 'virgins' like Betsy and Hylda both offer Esther a chilling vision of a possible future. She wants the security of a close relationship with a man, she wants children, but she demands too the same sexual rights and freedoms men enjoy, along with the same ability to construct a rewarding career in the public world which is not just that of serving men.

> My mother kept telling me that nobody wanted a plain English major. But an English major who knew shorthand was something else again. Everybody would want her. She would be in demand among all the up-and-coming young men and she would transcribe letter after thrilling letter.
>
> The trouble was, I hated the idea of serving men in any way. I wanted to dictate my own thrilling letters. (Plath 1966, 79)

It is no doubt for this reason that Esther considers Doreen's sexual freedom to be inadequate, for it still involves subservience to a man. Faced with the sordid reality of Doreen's drunken promiscuity, we see Esther hesitating between the two unsatisfactory and mutually exclusive alternatives, and choosing, rather half-heartedly at this stage, to become a 'virgin' rather than a 'whore'.

> I made a decision about Doreen that night. I decided I would watch her and listen to what she said, but deep down I would have nothing at all to do with her. Deep down, I would be loyal to Betsy and her innocent friends. It was Betsy I resembled at heart. (Plath 1966, 24)

We know, however, that Esther is trying here to persuade herself; she resembles Betsy about as much as she resembles Doreen, and her desperate attempt to find an identity for herself leads her like a shuttlecock from one unsatisfactory alternative to another. It is not accidental that at different times Esther adopts a false name – the ludicrously unsophisticated 'Elly Higginbottom'. Her incipient breakdown is revealed early on in the book when, Lenny (we presume) and Doreen are trying to get her up to let the drunken Doreen in:

> 'Elly, Elly, Elly,' the first voice mumbled, while the other voice went on hissing 'Miss Greenwood, Miss Greenwood, Miss Greenwood, Miss Greenwood', as if I had a split personality or something. (Plath 1966, 22)

'Elly' and 'Esther' (and perhaps 'Elaine', the heroine of the story Esther starts to write) represent the same social pressures that the 'two' Miss Hardcastles represent in Goldsmith's play. Elly Higginbottom is Esther's 'Betsy' character (we can recall that Betsy, in the New York group photograph, holds an ear of corn to show that she wants to be a farmer's wife).

> I thought if I ever did get to Chicago, I might change my name to Elly Higginbottom for good. Then nobody would know I had thrown up a scholarship at a big eastern women's college and mucked up a month in New York and refused a perfectly solid medical student for a husband who would one day be a member of the AMA and earn pots of money.
> In Chicago, people would take me for what I was.
> I would be simple Elly Higginbottom, the orphan. People would love me for my sweet, quiet nature. They wouldn't be after me to read books and write long papers on the twins in James Joyce. And one day I might just marry a virile, but tender, garage mechanic and have a big cowy family, like Dodo Conway. (Plath 1966, 140)

Esther's descent into breakdown involves a bouncing between these alternatives represented by the different figs on the tree, alternatives which, it needs stressing, are not just mutually exclusive but are also inadequate and unsatisfying in themselves.

Esther's frantic oscillation between being Elly Higginbottom and coolly deciding to lose her virginity is not, then, something that is indicative of an internal imbalance in her basic makeup; it is a response to the contradictory pressures that are placed upon her. It is worth stressing that although Esther is the one who breaks down, *all* the men she comes into contact with have exactly the same double standards with regard to women as oppress her. Eric, the student she talks to after he discovers that his date has eloped with a taxi driver, describes his initiation into sex with a prostitute in 'a notorious whore house':

> [. . .] he had her under a fly-spotted twenty-five watt bulb, and it was nothing like it was cracked up to be. It was boring as going to the toilet.
> I said maybe if you loved a woman it wouldn't seem so boring, but Eric said it would be spoiled by thinking this woman too was just an animal like the rest, so if he loved anybody he would never go to bed with her.

He'd go to a whore if he had to and keep the woman he loved free of all that dirty business. (Plath 1966, 82)

Esther considers that Eric might be a good person to go to bed with, as he had already done it and didn't seem dirty-minded or silly when he talked about it, but when he writes to her to say that he thought he might really be able to love her, she realizes that she is the type he would never go to bed with. Esther's rejection of the possibility of a sexual relationship with him, then, *follows* his indication that he himself splits girls into those he loves and those he sleeps with.

In much the same way, the woman-hating Marco divides the female sex into sluts and nuns, and brutally assaults Esther when she says that he will love some one else apart from the cousin who is going to be a nun. Esther's actual soiling here (Marco pushes her in the mud and soils her dress) is paralleled by the symbolic soiling of the mat Mrs Willard (Buddy's mother) makes from strips of wool taken from her husband's old suits. Esther says that she would have hung it on the wall after having spent weeks on it, but Mrs Willard puts it on the floor in place of her kitchen mat, 'and in a few days it was soiled and dull and indistinguishable from any mat you could buy for under a dollar in the Five and Ten.' The symbolic import of this is not lost upon Esther:

And I knew that in spite of all the roses and kisses and restaurant dinners a man showered on a woman before he married her, what he secretly wanted when the wedding service was ended was for her to flatten out underneath his feet like Mrs Willard's kitchen mat.

Hadn't my own mother told me that as soon as she and my father left Reno on their honeymoon – my father had been married before, so he needed a divorce – my father said to her, 'Whew, that's a relief, now we can stop pretending and be ourselves'? – and from that day on my mother never had a minute's peace. (Plath 1966, 88)

'Being oneself' is not only easier for a man in Esther's society, it also forces women to be what men want them to be. It is thus appropriate that after her soiling and assault at the hands of Marco Esther returns to her hotel and lets her clothes – the dirty ones stuffed under her bed by Doreen – drift out of the hotel window into the New York night. The action symbolizes Esther's rejection of the identity implied by 'all those uncomfortable, expensive clothes' that she mentions early on in the course of the novel, clothes which define her in a particular way for men, and for herself.

When Esther is taken by Buddy Willard to watch the birth of a baby, she is told by him that the woman is on a drug which will make her forget that she has had any pain. Ernest Hilgard writes on this phenomenon in his book on divided consciousness:

It is clinically reported that obstetric patients given thiopental may show signs of great anguish during the delivery, with verbal complaints as well, only to report after resting that the experience was pleasant and pleasurable throughout. There is some hint that only the anguish is unremembered (Editorial, *Lancet*, 1974). (Hilgard 1977, 71)

For Plath this clinical oddity clearly has a powerful symbolic force, and seems suggestive of something more general in the way men treat women. Esther, having been told of this drug by Buddy Willard, thinks that

it sounded just like the sort of drug a man would invent. Here was a woman in terrible pain, obviously feeling every bit of it or she wouldn't groan like that, and she would go straight home and start another baby, because the drug would make her forget how bad the pain had been, when all the time, in some secret part of her, that long, blind, doorless and windowless corridor of pain was waiting to open up and shut her in again. (Plath 1966, 68)

The drug, for Esther, symbolizes the way men force women to deny crucial aspects of their experience in order to conform with what men want them to be. And the denial is so effective that they convince themselves, all but that 'secret part' of themselves, that dissociated compartment in which the truth of their feelings is stored. The passage is interesting for a number of reasons, not least because it shows Plath using an example of drug-induced dissociation to represent larger, more social forms of female personality division.

In *The Bell Jar* all the men are hypocrites. I have mentioned Buddy Willard and Eric, and Esther's father. Consider too Irwin, who conceals Esther in his flat while he dissuades another woman from entering, and Doctor Gordon, whose family photograph displays a different personality from that implied by his memories of the wartime WAC station.

It is for this reason that two crucial elements in Esther's recovery are her gaining control over her own reproductive powers through visiting the clinic, and her getting Irwin to pay for her medical treatment.

'What I hate is the thought of being under a man's thumb,' I had told Doctor Nolan. 'A man doesn't have a worry in the world, while I've got a baby hanging over my head like a big stick, to keep me in line.' (Plath 1966, 234)

But while such achievements do constitute the gaining of a certain amount of freedom, Esther is aware that one does not escape from one's past, from the network of social relationships that one has experienced, that easily. Her self is not something that can be defined separately from her contacts with other people, from what they have expected of her, done to her, forced her to be:

I remembered the cadavers and Doreen and the story of the fig-tree and Marco's diamond and the sailor on the Common and Doctor Gordon's wall-eyed nurse and the broken thermometer and the negro with his two

kinds of beans and the twenty pounds I gained on insulin and the rock
that bulged between sky and sea like a grey skull.

Maybe forgetfulness, like a kind snow, should numb and cover them.
But they were part of me. They were my landscape. (Plath 1966, 250)

The Bell Jar is not, however, concerned merely to talk about the split personality forced on to women by men in an abstract and ahistorical way;
this theme is given a precise historical and social context in the novel, and
it thus meshes in with larger social and political concerns of Plath's, concerns all too clearly expressed in her writing but all too often ignored and
distorted.

Last Sunday . . . I had an immensely moving experience and attended
the arrival of the Easter weekend marchers from the atomic bomb plant at
Aldermaston to Trafalgar Square in London. [. . .] I found myself
weeping to see the tan, dusty marchers, knapsacks on their backs
– Quakers and Catholics, Africans and whites, Algerians and French
– 40 percent were London housewives. I felt proud that the baby's first
real adventure should be as a protest against the insanity of world-
annihilation. Already a certain percentage of unborn children are
doomed by fallout and no one knows the cumulative effects of what is
already poisoning the air and sea.

I hope, by the way, that neither you nor Warren will vote for Nixon.
His record is atrocious from his California campaign on – a Machiavelli
of the worst order. Could you find out if there is any way I can vote? I
never have and feel badly to be deprived of however minute a participa-
tion in political affairs. What do you think of Kennedy? The Sharpesville
massacres are causing a great stir of pity and indignation here. (Plath
1975, 378)

I quote this passage from Sylvia Plath's *Letters Home* at length, because it
seems to me to establish certain things about Plath which are too often
ignored or denied. Plath was, as she admitted in an interview given on the 30
October 1962, 'rather a political person' (Orr 1966, 169). That statement
comes two years after the comments quoted above, which were written in
April 1960 to her mother, but there is ample evidence to suggest that it is a
fair description of Plath during most of her adult life. The point needs to be
made because Plath has suffered overmuch from critics who have consistently reduced her work to the expression of a disturbed psyche, rather
than seeing it as a response to, and description of, the real social world in
which she lived. Responses to *Letters Home* were symptomatic in this
respect; many concentrated upon those parts of the letters which were concerned with discussions of clothes, of boy-friends, and of domestic detail.
Plath, it was suggested, turned out to be rather a boring, if not trivial, person
through the evidence of her letters. Her recurrent concern with politics was
all too often not mentioned at all.

But this split in the letters – between Plath the typical (or allegedly typical) young girl, concerned with the latest fashion or boy-friend, and gushing about her feelings about personal relationships, and Plath the serious young woman concerned with large political and social issues – is one for which Plath herself can hardly be blamed. Plath existed in a world in which stereotypical roles for women were tightly defined and were, in many cases, mutually exclusive. 'The female academic' (or poet), and 'the young woman enjoying her sexuality' were not roles that society considered to be at all compatible with each other. Approached with a historical sensitivity, Plath's work indicates an active intelligence at work to understand herself and her world as mutually interdependent entities. In her published comments upon her own work – especially her poetry – Plath is remarkably consistent, indicating whenever she is interviewed that her poems are intended to be about both the personal and the political, and indeed to be about the relationship and mutual dependence of the personal and the political. Is the following statement, for instance, one which could possibly legitimate a belief that she saw either the personal or the political as independent of the other?

> The issues of our time which preoccupy me at the moment are the incalculable genetic effects of fallout and a documentary article on the terrifying, mad, omnipotent marriage of big business and the military in America – 'Juggernaut, The Warfare State', by Fred. J. Cook in a recent *Nation*. Does this influence the kind of poetry I write? Yes, but in a sidelong fashion. [. . .] My poems do not turn out to be about Hiroshima, but about a child forming itself finger by finger in the dark. They are not about the terrors of mass extinction, but about the bleakness of the moon over a yew tree in a neighboring graveyard. [. . .]
>
> In a sense, these poems are deflections. I do not think they are an escape. For me, the real issues of our time are the issues of every time – the hurt and wonder of loving; making in all its forms – children, loaves of bread, paintings, buildings; and the conservation of life of all people in all places, the jeopardizing of which no abstract doubletalk of 'peace' or 'implacable foes' can excuse. (Plath 1980, 64)

That comes from an interview first published in February 1962; a few months later, on 30 October 1962, she gave another interview in which she confirmed this view of her work:

> I think my poems immediately come out of the sensuous and emotional experiences I have, but I must say that I cannot sympathize with these cries from the heart that are informed by nothing except a needle or a knife, or whatever it is. I believe that one should be able to control and manipulate experiences, even the most terrifying, like madness, being tortured, this sort of experience, and one should be able to manipulate these experiences with an informed and intelligent mind. I think that

personal experience is very important, but certainly it shouldn't be a kind of shut-box and mirror-looking, narcissistic experience. I believe it should be *relevant*, and relevant to the larger things, the bigger things such as Hiroshima and Dachau and so on. (Orr 1966, 169)

Plath's comments upon her work, then, suggest a keen appreciation of the complex relationship existing between the personal and the public; to approach her work as an expression merely of her internal tensions or difficulties – which in turn are seen as unrelated to anything outside of herself – is to deny that 'informed and intelligent mind' that was seeing these tensions and difficulties in the light of a complex set of relationships with 'the larger things.'

If we turn back to *The Bell Jar* we can see that the novel concerns itself not with a universalized sex-war, but with the complexities of human relationships in a very specific context.

It was a queer, sultry summer, the summer they electrocuted the Rosenbergs, and I didn't know what I was doing in New York. I'm stupid about executions. The idea of being electrocuted makes me sick, and that's all there was to read about in the papers – goggle-eyed headlines staring up at me on every street corner and at the fusty, peanut-smelling mouth of every subway. It had nothing to do with me, but I couldn't help wondering what it would be like, being burned alive all along your nerves.

I thought it must be the worst thing in the world. (Plath 1966, 1)

Although Esther Greenwood, rather disingenuously, tells us that 'It had nothing to do with me', we learn a few lines further on that she had heard so much about the Rosenbergs 'I couldn't get them out of my mind.' The novel thus opens with an act of legalized murder that is specifically related to the heroine's depression, and which later on is paralleled by her own treatment through electro-convulsive therapy. Objecting to being given ECT without having previously been warned, she asserts that had she been given such a warning

I would have gone down the hall between two nurses, past DeeDee and Loubelle and Mrs Savage and Joan, with dignity, like a person coolly resigned to execution. (Plath 1966, 224)

Through the subtle and economical use of symbol and image, a number of key associations are introduced to the reader in the first few pages of *The Bell Jar*.

I knew something was wrong with me that summer, because all I could think about was the Rosenbergs and how stupid I'd been to buy all those uncomfortable, expensive clothes, hanging limp as fish in my closet, and how all the little successes I'd totted up so happily at college fizzled to nothing outside the slick marble and plate-glass fronts along Madison Avenue.

I was supposed to be having the time of my life. (Plath 1966, 2)

The glass shop-front blends in with the image of the bell jar in the novel, and brings with it ideas of the alienating world of commerce and consumerism. It is the Madison Avenue world of New York from which Esther feels cut off, a world in which the people around her come to seem more and more dehumanized. The shop window image is picked up later in the novel when Esther visits Doctor Gordon's private hospital, and Esther tells us that

[. . .] I felt as if I were sitting in the window of an enormous department store. The figures around me weren't people, but shop dummies, painted to resemble people and propped up in attitudes counterfeiting life. (Plath 1966, 149)

And of course in that same hospital Esther receives the ECT treatment that calls to mind the execution of the Rosenbergs. Much later on in the novel the same complex of associations reappears, but this time linked to a particular image of mindless 'femininity' in the person of the chillingly brutal Hylda:

[Hylda] stared at her reflection in the glossed shop windows as if to make sure, moment by moment, that she continued to exist. The silence between us was so profound I thought part of it must be my fault.

So I said, 'Isn't it awful about the Rosenbergs?'

The Rosenbergs were to be electrocuted late that night.

'Yes!' Hylda said, and at last I felt I had touched a human string in the cat's cradle of her heart. It was only as the two of us waited in the tomb-like morning gloom of the conference room that Hylda amplified that Yes of hers.

'It's awful such people should be alive.' (Plath 1966, 105)

Such passages build up a family of associations as the novel progresses: the particular mindlessness of Hylda's self-regarding transformation of herself into a sort of beautiful but non-human object (in the group photograph she holds the 'bald, faceless head of a hatmaker's dummy to show she wanted to design hats'); the inhuman world of commerce and its objects cut off from Esther's humanity by the same sort of glass wall which forms her bell jar, and the larger significance of ritual terrorism and brutality involved in the Rosenbergs' execution. We can see here how what appears at first sight to be an essentially private trauma is related 'to the larger things, the bigger things such as Hiroshima and Dachau'.

A very similar cluster of associations is to be found in Plath's poem 'The Munich Mannequins', where the mannequins in a Munich shop window, 'Naked and bald in their furs', are related both to the feeling of arid sterility the persona of the poem feels, and also to the larger sterility of fascism. Like many of the poems of Plath's which touch on the topic of fascism, the poem draws a parallel between delusory attempts to achieve both individual, and racial, purity. Both attempts are seen to lead to blood – and thus symbolically in one case, violence. The terrible perfection of the childless persona leads to the blood flow of menstruation just as the Nazi theories of racial purity led to the shedding of blood in acts of violence and murder against those to whom impurity had to be attributed in order to define the purity of the elect.

This theme comes over most clearly in what is perhaps Plath's best known poem: 'Daddy'. Critical attention has often concentrated on the supposedly autobiographical elements in this poem – of which there clearly are plenty – but the connection with what Plath calls 'the larger things' is important. Indeed, what the poem demonstrates very strikingly is that we err if we imagine that the realm of personal relationships is constructed out of material untouched by wider social conflicts and contradictions. In this connection, a remarkable parallel can be drawn between this poem and the case history in *Sybil*. The author of the latter book tells us of Sybil that she

[. . .] had made identification with the Jews in German concentration camps. She thought of her mother as Hitler, the torturer, and of herself as a tortured Jew. (Schreiber 1975, 244)

In a note written for a BBC radio programme, Sylvia Plath said of 'Daddy' that it was

[. . .] a poem spoken by a girl with an Electra complex. Her father died while she thought he was God. Her case is complicated by the fact that her father was also a Nazi and her mother very possibly part Jewish. In the daughter the two strains marry and paralyse each other – she has to act out the awful little allegory once over before she is free of it. (quoted by M.L. Rosenthal in Newman 1970, 70)

Here racial mixing, as in Faulkner, symbolizes the internalization of the public brutalities of our, and our forefathers', age.

The pattern of *external* conflicts being transformed into an *internal* conflict in the individual and then *acted out* is, I feel, very suggestive. It describes exactly the sort of process that takes place in Sybil, and in other individuals who experience multiple personality states. But more than this, we need to note that the external conflict in this case is both a personal and a public one; it is both between the individual's mother and father, and between Nazi and Jew. Moreover, the poem attempts to relate the public and the personal in other ways, suggesting that the attractiveness of Nazi ideology and imagery to those taken in by it depends to a certain extent upon its making contact with powerful subjective sources of emotion such as sexual attractiveness. Put another way: the fact that the stereotypes of masculine sexual attractiveness in a given society resemble at least the outward forms of male-dominated political violence and repression in that, or other, societies is not accidental. Our images of the sexually attractive are not constructed in a purely biological manner; they relate to those images of masculinity and femininity given authority within a society in non-sexual areas. As I suggested when talking about *She Stoops to Conquer*, our perception of relationships of class and power is implicated in the subjective experience of sexuality.

> Every woman adores a Fascist,
> The boot in the face, the brute
> Brute heart of a brute like you.
> ('Daddy')

Thus I think that George Steiner is wrong to suggest that Sylvia Plath, in poems such as this, had no right 'to draw on the reserves of animate horror' of the Nazi period (Steiner 1969, 248). Steiner has suggested that Plath, who was not Jewish, was drawing upon the suffering of others to express a purely private pain. I have much sympathy for anyone who feels that the subject of the holocaust should not be exploited for cheap effect or to inject a spurious significance into essentially private pains. But I feel that Plath is trying to suggest links between these private pains and the 'larger things' of German fascism – much as Auden does in rather different ways in a poem such as 'Spain'.

Crucial to the establishment of this connection is the assertion that in a world dominated by violence and oppression, human sexuality cannot remain pure and unsullied by these forces. More particularly, where concepts of 'masculinity' are corrupted with ideas of power and violence, and where male sexuality is related to patriarchal power, then some conflation of 'the paternal' and 'the violent' will be found in the popular images of male sexual attractiveness. Like 'The Munich Mannequins' the poem suggests that there is more than a parallel between the 'private' and 'public' worlds portrayed – there is a connection. In both the Nazi persecution of the Jews and also in the incorporation of images of power and brutality in the stereotype of male sexual attractiveness we see *purity* and *violence* as two sides of the same coin. It is for this reason that German domesticity – 'The baby lace, the green-leaved confectionery' of 'The Munich Mannequins' – is seen as so sinister. It implies a violence necessary to maintain this sterile purity. As Plath reminds us,

> The snows of the Tyrol, the clear beer of Vienna
> Are not very pure or true.
> ('Daddy')

In order to assert the purity of the so-called Aryan race the Nazis had to persecute those defined as non-Aryan. In like manner the counterpart of the myth of female purity in our society's ideas concerning human sexuality is male violence. Thus in the poem, obsessed by the stereotypically fascist in men, the persona feels herself to be dehumanized, turned into an object. The reader may have been struck in the course of this book by the number of women who commit or attempt suicide. It is as if the divided women of Faulkner, Jean Rhys and Sylvia Plath are doomed to be destroyed when their internalized male force turns upon and pursues the repressed female in them.

There is another striking parallel between *Sybil* and the work of Plath. Plath was clearly obsessed by certain hospital images – of cadavers on the dissecting table, of babies in glass jars preserved in fluid. One of Sybil's personalities, Peggy Lou, tells her doctor that

> I went to the medical school museum, where I saw a brain of a forty-eight-year-old man with a bullet wound in his head and a brain of a thirty-eight-year-old woman who had had a stroke. And there were a lot of little babies in glass jars. Those jars were awful interesting. I had lots of fun in Philadelphia. (Schreiber 1975, 299)

In both cases what seems to lie at the root of the fascination is the idea of enclosure, an enclosure that turns the human being into an object. Plath's work is dominated by images of what can be called 'links' and 'enclosures', images which invariably raise the issue of the dependence of the individual and his or her sense of self upon other people. In many cases these images are related to another recurrent element in her work, what Marjorie Perloff has called a central paradox at the heart of her work – the fact that 'human beings are dead, inanimate, frozen, unreal, while everything that is non-human is intensely alive, vital, potent' (Perloff 1970, 57).

These aspects of her work are related to the purity/violence opposition. For the paradox that is often explored in her writings is that the more the individual tries to be him or herself exclusively ('purely', as Plath might have expressed it), the more dehumanized, objectified he or she becomes. The fact that all of these recurrent elements in Plath's work constitute a family can perhaps be illustrated by quoting from the book *Culture and Communication* by the anthropologist Edward Leach:

> Individuals do not live in society as isolated individuals with clear-cut boundaries; they exist as individuals inter-connected in a network by relations of power and domination. Power, in this sense, resides in the interfaces between individuals, in ambiguous boundaries. The logical paradox is that (i) I can only be completely sure of what I am if I cleanse myself of all boundary dirt, but (ii) a completely clean 'I' with no boundary dirt would have no interface relations with the outside world or with other individuals. Such an 'I' would be free from the domination of others but would in turn be wholly impotent. The inference is the opposition:
>
> clean/dirty = impotence/potency
>
> and hence that *power is located in dirt.* (Leach 1976, 62)

This perhaps explains why the idea of purity returns time and time again in Plath's work, but always associated with the idea of sterility, or of death. When Esther in *The Bell Jar* allows her dirty clothes to drift out of the hotel window she is cleansing herself, but at the same time risking impotence and objectification. In the same way, the Nazi persecution of the Jews seems to give Plath a horrifying example of the sterility and dehumanization consequent upon attempts to 'purify the race'.

Leach is a structuralist, and such structuralist approaches to the understanding of larger patterns of belief and behaviour can be very illuminating, but they have their limitations. In particular, their tendency to be ahistorical excludes the necessary question of why in a particular society the search for 'a completely pure "I" with no boundary dirt' should be sought so hard. Why should not people accept that their individuality, their identity, depend upon their relationships with other people? Again, why is it that the search for purity should not be universal, should apparently not dominate the consciousnesses of individuals in some societies?

To answer this it is instructive to think of the examples of Sybil and of Esther Greenwood, ignoring for the time being that one of them is a real person and the other a fictional character. It seems to me that both are fascinated by the escape offered, symbolically, by enclosure, because their connections with the outside world are contradictory and threatening. I have said that Plath's work is full of images of links and enclosures; more revealingly, the links are nearly always seen to be threatening, and the enclosures offer an escape that is, paradoxically, stifling. So far as the links are concerned, the image of *hooks* recurs very frequently in Plath's work; like the image of the moon it seems to draw a number of things together for her. Not only does it have associations of deformity, but it is the archetypal image of a threatening link, a link that offers to capture, hurt and subdue the individual. Revealingly, in the poem 'Tulips', smiles on the faces of husband and child in the bedside photograph are described as hooks: they represent potential human contact, with all its demands, for the hospitalized individual revelling in the freedom of her medical depersonalization. We can perhaps recall the way in which the contradictions of a business organization led Barbara O'Brien to an obsession with hooks and hook-men.

The same security in a depersonalizing purity is shown in 'Fever 103°', where again the isolation of the persona is at once purifying and sterilizing, culminating eventually in death. But here other associations in the poem are particularly relevant to our inquiry. Mention of radiation and of Hiroshima ash suggests that there are sound, objective reasons for the individual to feel scared of the outside world, to want to cut off connections with an objective reality that in certain ways is genuinely threatening. Further on in the same poem Plath has the persona of the poem describe herself as an expensive object:

> I am a lantern –
> My head a moon
> Of Japanese paper, my gold beaten skin
> Infinitely delicate and infinitely expensive.
> ('Fever 103°')

The poem thus suggests the depersonalizing force of commercialism, of the replacement of human valuation with cash or exchange value. It situates the desire for purity and, ultimately, extinction in a context in which real external threats such as nuclear weaponry (with which we know Plath was concerned, especially in terms of its effects upon the unborn), and objective forces of depersonalization exist. There seems little doubt that a term that the women's movement has given currency to – 'sex object' – would have met with Plath's approval, for her work constantly teases away at the means whereby stereotyped views of sexual attractiveness, and in particular the confusion of sexual attractiveness with monetary or commercial worth, dehumanize and reify the individual.

It seems that where there exist threatening external contradictions, then the individual becomes concerned with enclosure and frightened of connections; Wemmick lives in the country in a mock castle – even drawing a drawbridge up behind him when he enters it – and refuses to get to know Jaggers, his employer, beyond what is professionally required. Enclosures become attractive and terrifying, offering security from attack, but cutting off that which is life-giving. It is interesting that shoes are recurrently used by Plath to suggest death, in 'Daddy' and 'Berck Plage', for example. In the latter poem she writes

> This black boot has no mercy for anybody.
> Why should it, it is the hearse of a dead foot

In a book published in 1830, *The Philosophy of Sleep* by Robert Macnish, the author quotes from the dissociated utterances of a seventeen-year-old female.

> in her melancholy moments, she heard the bell, and then taking off one of her shoes as she sat upon the bed, 'I love the colour black,' says she; 'a little wider and a little longer, and even this might make me a coffin!' (Macnish 1830, 172)

The parallel suggests that the person harassed by contradictory pressures seeks enclosure but is simultaneously aware that it involves a rejection of life; symbols of enclosure (and the shoe is an obvious one) thus combine a fearful attractiveness with a sense of horrifying engulfment and extinction.

The bell jar, in the novel, is clearly one such image, with the additional element that it allows the imprisoned sufferer to see but not to connect with other people, and thus offers a convenient symbol for the sense of conscious exclusion from human intercourse that the mentally ill individual suffers from. In his *The Divided Self* R.D. Laing quotes a schizophrenic patient, Joan, who explains

> When I was catatonic, I tried to be dead and grey and motionless. I thought mother would like that. She could carry me around like a doll.
> I felt as though I were in a bottle. I could feel that everything was outside and couldn't touch me. (Laing 1966, 176)

Such images seem to occur naturally to those faced with the contradictions experienced by Joan here, or Esther in *The Bell Jar*; we do not need to concoct theories of influence to explain them.

Joan, in the quote from Laing, describes herself as a 'doll'. In 'The Applicant' Plath paints a grotesque transformation of the process of marriage into the language of various forms of reification, in which the insistence on the body as object implies a more general treatment of the person as object. In it, the prospective bride is described as

> A living doll, everywhere you look.
> It can sew, it can cook,
> It can talk, talk, talk.
>   ('The Applicant')

The poem must have been written soon after the song 'Living Doll' was popular, and it is capable of such a relentless exploration of the dehumanization of particular attitudes to marriage precisely because it considers the full implications of referring to a woman as a doll.

This sort of dehumanizing of women is perhaps investigated most effectively in the poém 'Lady Lazarus', the force of which comes from its insistence upon the relationship between the persona's suicide attempts and more recognizably conventional views of women as objects; in both cases it is the denial of life, the dehumanization that is, shockingly, exposed as a common factor. Thus the woman in the poem is an object of display:

> The peanut-crunching crowd
> Shoves in to see
>
> Them unwrap me hand and foot –
> The big strip tease.
>   ('Lady Lazarus')

Her dehumanization in death is comparable to the dehumanization of the strip-tease artist, seen as object not as human being. The larger relationships in the poem called up through various images and references – the Nazi/Jew, Doctor/patient ones – similarly bespeak treatment by men of women as objects rather than as people. And the stunningly ironic insistence on the commercial value of her wounds repeats the same message

> And there is a charge, a very large charge
> For a word or a touch
> Or a bit of blood
>
> Or a piece of my hair or my clothes.
> ('Lady Lazarus')

One important element in *The Bell Jar* is Plath's perception of the dehumanizing effect of commercial medicine; Joan tells Esther that she could see the dollar signs in her psychiatrist's eyes, and shortly after this a nurse tells Esther that when she has earned enough money to buy a car, she will clear out and take on only private cases (Plath 1966, 221). The nurse's behaviour is classically contradictory: her friendly conversation implies that she sees the patients as human beings, but what she actually says implies that she sees them only as means to an end, defines them only in cash terms.

Plath's sense of the threatening nature of human connections doubtless owes much to aspects of her personal biography; she repeatedly talks of the traumatic effect on her of her father's death when she was nine, and in the fragment *Ocean 1212-W* (significantly this is a telephone number – a link) she talks of the similar, earlier effect of learning that she had had a brother:

> Hugging my grudge, ugly and prickly, a sad sea urchin, I trudged off on my own, in the opposite direction toward the forbidding prison. As from a star I saw, coldly and soberly, the *separateness* of everything. I felt the wall of my skin: I am I. That stone is a stone. My beautiful fusion with the things of this world was over. (Plath 1980, 23)

The relationship between an external threat and a sense of purified but nonetheless diminished identity is surely clearly indicated here. In spite of this feeling of dehumanization, connection with the world of separate objects is seen as threatening, for it may once again betray, hurt. Plath's desire to link up personal experience with 'the larger things, the bigger things' is, then, generally successful. The use of images of racial persecution, sexism and commercialism remind us again that it is not just within the family that contradictory double-binds are generated for the individual – and that even within the family such tensions are linked to larger contradictions in the wider society.

My treatment of Plath's poems in terms of their larger themes and patterns of meaning is, I am conscious, a partial one. It tends to remove from sight what is crucial to any full understanding of her poetry: the sense of assertive life that springs from the vitality of her poetic expression. One of the curious paradoxes of Plath's later poetry is that for all its concern with neurosis, non-being, isolation and extinction; a fierce sense of life-affirming forcefulness is the predominant impression created by the poems. Behind the words, we are made aware, is a single, unitary consciousness demanding recognition of her existential claims. However battered the persona of the poem is, she is living, vital and *there*. The poems thus enact a representative struggle – between the forces of division and obliteration on the one hand, and the forces of integrity and commitment to living on the other. The poem is both the site and the occasion of the battle between these warring forces.

This sense of vital life comes, I think, from the polemical effect on the reader of the use Plath makes of direct statement in the poems, a statement that gathers force partly from its almost incantatory repetitiveness (as in the closing lines of 'Fever 103°'), and partly from the deliberate paring down of these statements to an almost parodically factual, 'unemotional' level.

Moreover, the concreteness of Plath's images gives an edge to the poems which is sharpened by the jolting effect of her use of taboo words and topics. There is nothing comfortable in these poems for the reader, they are full of the sharp edges of life with their padding of familiarity torn off. It is as if a 'silent observer' in the brain, watching the persona's dominant personality being drugged, denied and reified, is spitting abuse at the forces responsible for this existential murder.

It is for this reason that, in the last resort, these poems seem to me to assert an essential humanity, a belief in the wonder and oneness of the human personality, and a contempt for all that would deny this. 'Out of the ash' of this terrible poetry an undeniable humanity arises.

Conclusion

The main argument of this book – and the link between the case-histories and the literary analyses – is the claim that if an individual is brought up, and has to survive, in an environment constituted by contradictory systems of value, then he or she will become internally divided unless the external contradictions are clearly recognized. I think that the literary works make more explicit the links which join the realm of the private to the wider society: Sylvia Plath, for instance, states quite explicitly her intention to investigate connections between 'personal experience' and 'the larger things'. To a greater or lesser extent, however, this project is implicit in the creative inquiries of all the writers at whose work we have looked. The novelist and the dramatist cannot avoid looking at such relationships because the justifying impulse behind the novel and the drama is, to a large extent, a contextualizing one. The novel or play has to situate its characters, their actions and relationships, in a set of interlocking contexts which, unless the work is to meander into formalistic or ultra-modernist irrelevance, must be shown in significant interaction with them. By exposing such connections the writer is, I would argue, only making apparent that which is concealed or ignored in much of everyday life.

There are many different ways in which writers of different periods and societies can respond to the internal division of human beings, a division which I have suggested has become more acute during the modern age. The writer can devote increasing interest to the inner world of characters through the development of techniques such as the internal monologue and dialogue, and the stream-of-consciousness narrative. Alternatively he or she can project such inner conflicts outwards, objectifying them in doubles, parallel characters, and so on. But the writer cannot ignore this issue (and this is, in part, the answer to those suspicious of the validity of literary evidence so far as changes in human personality are concerned). He or she cannot ignore the issue because to do so is to abandon the exploration of the complexities of the relationship between personal relationships and the various social contexts that provide his or her fictional setting – and such an abandonment spells death for the literary work concerned.

On the evidence both of our case-histories and of the literary analyses we can suggest that social tensions, divisions between individuals, become internalized and result in divisions within individuals. And these internalized conflicts can then, in their turn, be projected back into society by means of contradictory forms of behaviour. The dialectical relationship between subjective and objective states is thus extremely complicated. It is as if human beings in a divided society have each a fifth column within them, representing those destructive forces in society which have insinuated themselves into the hearts and minds of individual human beings.

But in all this I believe that the drive for unity is powerful and consistent. In spite of the fact that division, contradiction, deceit all may have the advantage of offering temporary gains, limited survival value, human beings seem to strive to be undivided: the pressure of the truly human is towards the fighting out of contradictions and the establishment of internal consistency both within society and within the individual. Just as the classless society has, explicitly or implicitly, been what untold generations have sought for centuries, so too has the establishment of a world of undivided individuals represented a humanist ideal. The important thing is to realize that the two are linked, and that only by establishing a society that is undivided, in a world that is undivided, can there be human individuals free from hypocrisy and duplicity.

Bibliography

Allen, I.M. 1932: Somnambulism and dissociation of personality. *British Journal of Medical Psychology* **XI**.

Allison, Ralph B. 1974: A guide to parents: how to raise your daughter to have multiple personalities. *Family Therapy* **I**.

Auerbach, Erich 1971: *Mimesis: the representation of reality in western literature*. Trans. Willard R. Trask. Third printing. Princeton, NJ: Princeton University Press.

Bazin, Nancy Topping 1973: *Virginia Woolf and the androgynous vision*. New Jersey: Rutgers University Press.

B.C.A. 1908: My life as a dissociated personality. *Journal of Abnormal Psychology* **3** (October/November).

Bettelheim, Bruno 1961: *Paul and Mary*. New York: Anchor Books/Doubleday.

Bloch, Ernst; Lukács, Georg; Brecht, Bertolt; Benjamin, Walter; and Adorno, Theodor 1977: *Aesthetics and politics*. London: New Left Books.

Brontë, Charlotte 1981: *Villette*. Edited by Mark Lilly. Reprinted. Harmondsworth: Penguin Books.

Brontë, Emily 1975: *Wuthering Heights*. Edited by David Daiches. Reprinted. Harmondsworth: Penguin Books.

Chase, Robert Howland 1918: *The ungeared mind*. Philadelphia: F.A. Davis Co.

Coleman, Stanley M. 1934: The phantom double. *British Journal of Medical Psychology* **XIV**.

Congdon, M.H.; Hain, J. and Stevenson, I. 1961: A case of multiple personality illustrating the transition from role playing. *Journal of Nervous and Mental Diseases* **132**.

Conrad, Joseph 1966: *The secret sharer*. In *'Twixt land and sea*. Reprinted. London: Dent.

Cory, Charles E. 1919: Patience Worth. *Psychological Review* **26 (5)**.

— 1920: A divided self. *Journal of Abnormal Psychology* **14**.

Cutler, B. and Reed, J. 1975: Multiple personality: a single case study with a 15 year follow-up. *Psychological Medicine* **5**.

Cutten, George B. 1903: The case of John Kinsel. *Psychological Review* **X (5)**.

Dailey, Abram H. 1894: *Mollie Fancher, the Brooklyn enigma: an authentic statement of facts in the life of Mary J. Fancher, the psychological marvel of the nineteenth century.* Brooklyn, New York: Eagle Book Printing Department.

Dana, Professor Charles L., M.D. 1894: The study of a case of amnesia or 'double consciousness.' *Psychological Review* **1 (5)**.

De Quincey, Thomas 1908: *The confessions of an English opium-eater.* London: Dent.

Dewar, H., M.D., F.R.S. 1823: On uterine irritation and its effects on the female constitution. *Transactions of the Royal Society of Edinburgh* **IX**.

Dickens, Charles 1972: *Great expectations.* Reprinted. Harmondsworth: Penguin Books.

— 1982: *The mystery of Edwin Drood.* Edited with an introduction and notes by Margaret Cardwell. Oxford: Oxford University Press (the World's Classics).

Dostoyevsky, Fyodor 1958: *The brothers Karamazov.* Volume 1. Trans. David Magarshack. Harmondsworth: Penguin Books.

— 1972: *Notes from underground and the double.* Trans. Jessie Coulson. Harmondsworth: Penguin Books.

— 1974: *Crime and punishment.* Trans. David Magarshack. Reprinted. Harmondsworth: Penguin Books.

Eagleton, Terry 1975: *Myths of power.* London: Macmillan.

Ellenberger, Henri F. 1970: *The discovery of the unconscious: the history and evolution of dynamic psychiatry.* London: Allen Lane.

Erickson, M.H., and Kubie, L.S. 1939: The permanent relief of an obsessional phobia by means of communication with an unsuspected dual personality. *Psychoanalytic Quarterly* **8**.

Faulkner, William 1960: *Absalom, Absalom!.* Uniform edition. London: Chatto & Windus.

Finkelstein, Sidney 1968: *Existentialism and alienation in American literature.* Third printing. New York: International Publishers.

Frank, Joseph 1977: *Dostoyevsky: The seeds of revolt.* London: Robson Books.

Franz, S.I. 1933: *Persons one and three.* New York: McGraw-Hill.

Freud, Sigmund and Breuer, Joseph 1978: *Studies on hysteria.* Trans. James and Alix Strachey. Edited by James and Alix Strachey, assisted by Angela Richards. Reprinted. Harmondsworth: Penguin Books.

Friedman, Arthur (ed.) 1966: *Collected works of Oliver Goldsmith.* Volume five. Oxford: Clarendon Press.

Gaskell, Elizabeth 1979: *North and south.* Edited by Dorothy Collin. Reprinted. Harmondsworth: Penguin Books.

Goddard, Henry Herbert N.D. ?1927: *Two souls in one body? A case of dual personality.* London: Rider & Company.

Gruenewald, Doris 1971: Hypnotic techniques without hypnosis in the treatment of dual personality. *Journal of Mental and Nervous Diseases* **153 (1)**

Hawthorne, Nathaniel 1970: *Selected tales and sketches*. Third edition. San Francisco: Rinehart Press.

Hilgard, Ernest 1977: *Divided consciousness: multiple controls in human thought and action*. Chichester and New York: John Wiley.

Hodgson, Richard 1891: A case of double consciousness. *Society for Psychical Research Proceedings* 7.

Irwin, John T. 1975: *Doubling and incest/repetition and revenge: a speculative reading of Faulkner*. Baltimore and London: Johns Hopkins University Press.

Kaplan, Fred 1975: *Dickens and mesmerism: the hidden springs of fiction*. Princeton: Princeton University Press.

Keppler, C.F. 1972: *The literature of the second self*. Tucson Arizona: The University of Arizona Press.

Kohlenberg, Robert J. 1973: Behavioristic approach to multiple personality: a case study. *Behavior Therapy* 4.

Krag, Erik 1976: *Dostoyevsky: the literary artist*. Trans. Per Syversen. Oslo: Universitetsforlaget.

Laing, R.D. 1965: *The divided self*. Reprinted. Harmondsworth: Penguin Books.

Lancaster, Evelyn, and Poling, James 1958: *Strangers in my body*. London: Secker & Warburg.

Leach, Edward 1976: *Culture and communication*. London: Cambridge University Press.

Leont'ev, A.N. 1978: *Activity, consciousness and personality*. Trans. Marie J. Hall. Englewood Cliffs, NJ: Prentice-Hall.

Ludwig, Arnold M.; Brandsma, Jeffrey M.; Wilbur, Cornelia B.; Bedfeldt, Fernando; and Jameson, Douglas H. 1972: The objective study of a multiple personality. *Archives of General Psychology* 26 (April).

Lukács, Georg 1963: *The meaning of contemporary realism*. Trans. John and Necke Mander. London: Merlin Press.

Luria, A.R. 1976: *Cognitive development*. Trans. Martin Lopez-Morillas and Lynn Solotaroff. Edited by Michael Cole. Cambridge, Mass. and London: Harvard University Press.

Macnish, Robert 1830: *The philosophy of sleep*. Glasgow: W.R.M'Phun.

Massey, Irving 1976: *The gaping pig: literature and metamorphosis*. Berkeley and London: University of California Press.

Mikesell, William H. 1950: *Modern abnormal psychology*. New York: McLeod.

Miller, Arthur 1968: *Death of a salesman*. Reprinted. Harmondsworth: Penguin Books.

Murphy, Gardner 1966: *Personality: a biosocial approach to origins and structure*. Reissued with a new preface. New York and London: Basic Books.

Myoshi, Masao 1969: *The divided self: a perspective on the literature of the Victorians*. London: University of London Press.

Newman, Charles (ed.) 1970: *The art of Sylvia Plath: a symposium*. London: Faber & Faber.

O'Brien, Barbara 1976: *Operators and things: the inner life of a schizophrenic*. Reissued. London: Abacus.

Orr, Peter (ed.) 1966: *The poet speaks: interviews with contemporary poets*. London: Routledge & Kegan Paul.

Osgood, Charles E.; Luria, Z.; Jeans, R.F.; and Smith, S.W. 1976: The three faces of Evelyn: a case report. *Journal of Abnormal Psychology* **85(3)** (June).

Perloff, Marjorie 1970: Angst and animism in the poetry of Sylvia Plath. *Journal of Modern Literature* **1(1)**.

Plath, Sylvia 1955: *The magic mirror: a study of the double in two of Dostoevsky's novels*. Thesis submitted in partial fulfillment of the Special Honours in English. Northampton, Mass.: Smith College.

— 1965: *Ariel*. Fourth impression. London: Faber & Faber.

— 1966: *The bell jar*. Reprinted. London: Faber & Faber.

— 1975: *Letters home*. London: Faber & Faber.

— 1980: *Johnny Panic and the bible of dreams*. American edition with different content from British edition. New York: Harper & Row.

Plumer, Rev. William S., DD 1860: Mary Reynolds: a case of double consciousness. *Harpers New Monthly Magazine* **20**.

Prince, Morton 1906: *The dissociation of a personality: a biographical study in abnormal psychology*. London and New York: Longmans, Green & Co.

— 1914: *The unconscious: the fundamentals of human personality normal and abnormal*. New York: Macmillan.

— 1929: *Clinical and experimental studies in personality*. Cambridge, Mass.: Sci-Art Publishers.

— 1975: *Psychotherapy and multiple personality: selected essays*. Edited by Nathan G. Hale Jr. Cambridge, Mass.: Harvard University Press.

Rank, Otto 1979: *The double: a psychoanalytic study*. Translated and with an introduction by Harry Tucker Jr, New York and London: New American Library/Meridian Book.

Rhys, Jean 1968: *Wide Sargasso Sea*. Harmondsworth: Penguin Books.

— 1969: *Good morning, midnight*. Reissued. Harmondsworth: Penguin Books.

— 1971: *After leaving Mr Mackenzie*. Reissued. Harmondsworth: Penguin Books.

Rogers, Robert 1970: *The double in literature*. Detroit: Wayne State University Press.

Schatzman, Morton 1980: *The story of Ruth*: London: Duckworth.

Schreiber, Flora Rheta 1975: *Sybil*. Harmondsworth: Penguin Books.

Schwarz, Gary and Merten, Don; (with Fran Behan and Allyne Rosenthal) 1980: *Love and commitment*. Beverly Hills and London: Sage.

Sidis, Boris and Goodhart, Simon P. 1905: *Multiple personality*. New York: D. Appleton & Company.

Steiner, George 1969: In extremis. *Cambridge Review* **90** (February 7).

Steiner, Joan E. 1980: Conrad's 'The Secret Sharer': complexities of the doubling relationship. *Conradiana* **XII(3)**.

Stevenson, Robert Louis 1980: *Dr Jekyll and Mr Hyde and other tales*. Reprinted. London and New York: Dent/Dutton.

Stoller, Robert J. 1974: *Splitting: a case of female masculinity*. London: The Hogarth Press.

Taylor, W.S. and Martin, M.F. 1944: Multiple personality. *Journal of Abnormal and Social Psychology* **39(3)**.

Thigpen, Corbett H. and Cleckley, Hervey 1954: A case of multiple personality. *Journal of Abnormal and Social Psychology* **49(1)** (January).

— 1957: *The three faces of Eve*. London: Secker & Warburg.

Tuke, D. Hack (ed.) 1892: *A dictionary of psychological medicine*. Volume one. London: J. & A. Churchill.

Tymms, Ralph 1949: *Doubles in literary psychology*. Cambridge: Bowes & Bowes.

Vygotsky, L.S. 1978: *Mind in society*. Edited by Michael Cole. Vera John-Steiner, Sylvia Scribner & Ellen Souberman. Cambridge, Mass. and London: Harvard University Press.

Wellek, René (ed.) 1962: *Dostoyevsky: a collection of critical essays*. Englewood Cliffs, NJ: Prentice-Hall.

Wholey, Cornelius C. 1933: A case of multiple personality. *American Journal of Psychiatry* **XII(4)** (January).

Woolf, Virginia 1966: *Night and day*. Reprinted. London: Hogarth Press.

— 1967: The new biography. In *Collected essays*. Volume four. London: Hogarth Press.

— 1981: *Moments of being: unpublished autobiographical writings*. Edited with an introduction and notes by Jeanne Schulkind. Reprinted. Frogmore, St Albans: Triad/Granada.

Index